£375

General Editor: M. Rolf Ols

GU91007634

TAVISTOCK LIBR.
SOCIAL WORK PRACTICE

The Residential
Solution

25

The Residential Solution

State alternatives to family care

ANN DAVIS

TAVISTOCK PUBLICATIONS
London and New York

First published in 1981 by
Tavistock Publications Ltd
11 New Fetter Lane, London EC4P 4EE
Published in the USA by
Tavistock Publications
in association with Methuen, Inc.
733 Third Avenue, New York, NY 10017

Photoset by Rowland Phototypesetting Ltd
Bury St Edmunds, Suffolk
and printed in Great Britain by
Richard Clay (The Chaucer Press) Ltd
Bungay, Suffolk

British Library Cataloguing in Publication Data

Davis, Ann
The residential solution. – (Tavistock library
of social work practice)
1. Institutional care – Great Britain
I. Title
361'.05   HV59

ISBN 0-422-77320-4
ISBN 0-422-77330-1 Pbk

Contents

General editor's foreword

Tavistock Library of Social Work Practice is a new series of books primarily written for practitioners and students of social work and the personal social services, but also for those who work in the allied fields of health, education, and other public services. The series represents the collaborative effort of social work academics, practitioners, and managers. In addition to considering the theoretical and philosophical debate surrounding the topics under consideration, the texts are firmly rooted in practice issues and the problems associated with the organization of the services. Therefore the series will be of particular value to undergraduate and post-graduate students of social work and social administration.

The series was prompted by the growth and increasing importance of the social services in our society. Until recently there has been a general approbation of social work, reflected in a benedictory increase in manpower and resources, which has led to an unprecedented expansion of the personal social services, a proliferation of the statutory duties placed upon them, and major reorganization. The result has been the emergence of a profession faced with the immense responsibilities of promoting individual and social betterment, and bearing a primary responsibility to advocate on behalf of individuals and groups who do not always fulfil or respect normal social expectations of behaviour. In spite of the growth in services these tasks are often carried out with inadequate resources, an uncertain knowledge base, and as yet unresolved difficulties associated with the reorganization of the personal social services in 1970. In recent years these difficulties have been compounded by a level of criticism unprecedented since the Poor Law. The anti-social work critique has fostered some improbable alliances between groups of social administrators, sociologists, doctors, and the media, united in their belief that social work has failed in its general obligation to 'provide services to the people', and in its particular duty to socialize the delinquent, restrain parents who abuse their children, prevent old people from dying alone, and provide a satisfactory level of community care for the sick, the chronically handicapped, and the mentally disabled.

These developments highlight three major issues that deserve particular attention. First, is the need to construct a methodology for analysing social and personal situations and prescribing action; second, is the necessity to apply techniques that measure the performance of the individual worker and the profession as a whole in meeting stated objectives; third, and outstanding, is the requirement to develop a knowledge base against which the needs of clients are understood and decisions about their care are taken. Overall, the volumes in this series make explicit and clarify these issues; contribute to the search for the distinctive knowledge base of social work; increase our understanding of the aetiology and care of personal, familial, and social problems; describe and explore new techniques and practice skills; aim to raise our commitment towards low status groups which suffer public, political, and professional neglect; and to promote the enactment of comprehensive and socially just policies. Above all, these volumes aim to promote an understanding which interprets the needs of individuals, groups, and communities in terms of the synthesis between inner needs and the social realities that impinge upon them, and which aspire to develop informed and skilled practice.

M. ROLF OLSEN
Birmingham University
1981

For John and Marie Betteridge

Acknowledgements

During the years it has taken me to complete this book I have been helped by innumerable friends and colleagues. Those I mention here are the friends who gave me a great deal during the final 'burst'. Many thanks go to Kevin Finnegan, Gayle Foster, Jo Pearce, and Dave Towell who responded with criticism and encouragement to an erratic flow of drafts; to Margaret Fletcher and Bobby Spice who not only transformed my original scribblings into a manuscript but also raised my spirits on many occasions; to Ted Archer for his work on the references; and to Alex Davis who nagged, encouraged, and criticized in sufficient quantities to keep me 'at it'. I know he is as relieved as I am at the prospect of living without this 'lodger'.

1

The boundaries of residential social work

The provision of care and control in residential institutions is a feature of a number of British welfare services. The penal service, the health service, the education service, and the personal social services have all developed various forms of residential provision; social workers find themselves involved with them all. How social workers become involved in implementing residential solutions depends on where the prime responsibility for providing the residential service lies. Social workers based in hospitals and prisons supplement what is essentially medical or penal care, but those based in an elderly persons' home or childrens' home are directly responsible for determining and providing the care offered to residents.

Once this distinction is made, it is still difficult to draw a clear boundary around that sector of residential care which is the prime responsibility of social work. It is a territory open to dispute for a number of reasons.

First, the area covered is still relatively new to social work and the profession is uncertain how to relate to it (Payne 1977). Residential institutions have been seen by some as 'settings' in which the methods of social work (i.e. casework and groupwork) can be practised. Others have adopted the view that residential work is a distinct method of social work along with casework, groupwork, and community work. For yet others it has been the distinctive needs of the client group, rather than the approach of the profession, which give residential care its identity.

The working party set up by the Central Council for Education and

2   The Residential Solution

Training in Social Work (CCETSW), reporting in 1973, examined this question in detail. It concluded that the only differences between residential work and other social work specializations were 'technical'; residential work was a part of the social work profession because it held values, objectives, and clients in common with other social work services and because it drew on the same knowledge and skills. The working party therefore recommended a single pattern of training for field and residential social workers in Great Britain (CCETSW 1973).

These conclusions are now having very real consequences for the kind of training being offered to residential social workers, but they have not resolved the debate about the nature of their work. Indeed, a new dimension to the debate has been introduced by the 'unitary' or 'integrated' approach to social work training adopted on some courses. This approach views social work practice as 'system-centred' rather than 'method-centred'. From this point of view:

> 'residential work requires all the knowledge and skills of social work. Nevertheless we find it difficult to conceptualize residential work as a "methodological specialization" . . . our view is that residential work is part of an open system which is in continuing exchange with its related environment.'   (Payne 1977 : 213)

A second important factor in this discussion of territory is that, whatever is said or written about the skills and values of workers in residential care, only 4 per cent of them have had a professional social work training (Walton and Elliott 1980 : 21). In addition, many work in establishments headed by individuals with teaching or nursing qualifications, or in establishments pushed very reluctantly under the social work umbrella by changes in legislation. As a result, many residential care practices owe more to the influence of history and other professional approaches than they do to social work.

Recent research has shown that a number of Community Homes with Education (a creation of the 1969 Children and Young Persons Act which integrated residential care for delinquents with that for deprived children) still demonstrate a primary concern with education and training, rather than with child care (Cawson 1978). Many of our elderly persons' homes continue to draw heavily on a medical-custodial approach to care whose origins are to be found in decades of workhouse and hospital provision (DHSS 1979). Moreover, while some children and disabled are cared for in homes which do not differ physically from others in their street, many find themselves in large establishments standing in their own grounds – products of an era in which residential care was concerned with protecting the community from deviant groups.

Related to this lack of a common and distinctive approach to practice is a third boundary problem, which Payne identifies:

'If the client groups in residential care are examined, we find thousands of children and adults living in psychiatric and mental subnormality hospitals, not because they need medical care and treatment, but because alternative resources are unavailable. However, responsibility for the care of these people, whose needs are primarily personal and social and not medical, lies with staff whose training is in hospital work rather than social.'

(Payne 1977 : 207)

In other words, the boundaries of residential social work are blurred because, viewed from the perspective of the personal and social needs of clients, they overlap with areas claimed by other professional groups.

Finally, this sector of residential care has no administrative unity. While many establishments are part of local authority social service departments, a sizeable number are the responsibility of voluntary and private organizations and the probation service. In each of these services residential care has its own place in an overall pattern of resources being offered. For each, distinct policies towards staffing, organization, and finance of residental establishments have, as Tizard and others have shown (Tizard, Sinclair, and Clarke 1975), a unique impact on the residential experiences of both staff and residents.

The basis, then, on which a boundary has been drawn around the territory of residential social work, appears to be nothing more than an aspiration to provide a form of residential care which is shaped primarily by social work values, objectives, and skills. This aspiration appears to have been promoted as much by post-war changes in welfare policy and legislation as it has by the interest of the social work profession. Its connection with the current daily experiences of the majority of staff and residents in residential units remains tenuous.

4   The Residential Solution

From the CCETSW working party a definition of this aspiration emerged as: 'a method of social work in which a team of social workers operates together with a group of residents to create a living environment designed to enhance the functioning of individual residents in the context of their total environment' (CCETSW 1973). This is a definition which succeeds in clearing some ground, only to raise more questions than it answers; for, in the light of both current practice and future aspiration, terms such as 'team', 'operates', 'enhance', and 'functioning' require a great deal of elaboration. What does it mean to talk about 'a team of social workers' in situations where residential staff feel isolated from fieldworkers and managers and thirty-three out of every hundred remain in one establishment for less than a year? (Berry 1975). How valid is it to talk about 'enhancing the functioning of individual residents' when much of the knowledge we have about residential environments suggests that there is a tendency to damage rather than enhance individual functioning? (Walton and Elliott 1980 : 4).

Like so much of the professional discussion about residential social work, this definition reflects a view of the potential of residential care which contrasts sharply with past and current experience of this kind of intervention. Yet the gulf between aspiration and practice does not prevent continuing claims being made for the territorial expansion of residential social work.

During the 1970s a number of Department of Health and Social Security (DHSS) policy documents argued that substantial proportions of elderly, mentally ill, and physically handicapped patients need social work rather than health service residential care. In 1979 the Jay Committee, reviewing the residential care of the mentally handicapped, recommended that social work training should replace nurse training in this field. The arguments used emphasized that residential care for such groups should be primarily concerned with their 'individual' and 'social' needs and that an approach grounded in social work, rather than medicine, was best able to provide this.

Residential workers interested in discovering what they offer which can transform deprived living situations and meet the needs of such a wide array of individuals, will have difficulty in finding a satisfactory answer. The professional literature to date has focused mainly on residential work with particular client groups, and has not been concerned with the broad sweep of what has been described as 'a way of offering a client an opportunity for evaluating personal and social situations within a supportive environment' (Ward 1977). The reasons for this have already been touched upon. Drawing boundaries around residential social work is at present an act of faith, not an acknowledgement of a recognized and common identity; much needs to be done to arrive at some understanding of the potential and limitations of this social work strategy.

Residential social work is not, of course, alone in facing problems of identity. The last decade or so has witnessed a great deal of speculation, uncertainty, and controversy about the nature of social work (Brake and Bailey 1980 : 86). The special problem which residential social workers face is one of understanding the nature of the distinctive contribution they make. To do this they must look at the similarities and differences they have, not only with other social workers, but also with other workers (paid and unpaid) who are engaged in 'the daily care of dependent people'.

This chapter considers the issue of identity further by looking first at the route by which a sector of British residential care arrived in social work territory and, second, at the current estimates of the helping potential of residential social work.

The roots of residential social work

As one of the oldest forms of statutory welfare provision in Great Britain, residential care has a history which can be traced back to the Elizabethan Poor Relief Acts. Although policy and legislation in itself says little about the reality of residential care provided at any time, it is interesting to note the kind of solutions which this form of care was seen as offering to the social and economic problems of sixteenth-century England. The 1598 Act distinguished three types of potential inmate: the 'impotent' whose condition of destitution and disability required 'abiding places'; the 'able-bodied' who required 'workhouses' to combat their idleness; and the 'recalcitrant able-bodied' who required 'houses of correction' which would combine work and discipline in sufficient proportions to re-establish work habits (Checkland 1974 : 12).

Over two hundred years later a review of the operation of these Poor Laws showed that, where institutional provision did exist, it did not reflect such distinctions. Workhouses were offering residence to a range of people whose one common characteristic was destitution. A typical town workhouse of the early 1830s was occupied as follows:

> 'by sixty or eighty paupers, made up of a dozen or more neglected children (under the care, perhaps, of a pauper); about twenty or thirty able-bodied adult paupers of both sexes, and probably an equal number of aged and impotent persons. Amidst these the mothers of bastard children and prostitutes live without shame and associate freely with the youth, who have also the examples and conversation of the frequent inmates of the county gaol, the poacher, the vagrant, the decayed beggar. . . . To these may often be added a solitary blind person, one or two idiots and not infrequently are heard from among the rest, the incessant ravings of some neglected lunatic. In such receptacles the sick poor are often immured.'   (Checkland 1974 : 425)

Legislation which followed the report of the Royal Commission on the Poor Law (the 1834 Poor Law Amendment Act) was primarily concerned to deter the destitute from seeking help from the state. Central to this policy of deterrence was residential provision. The workhouse was given the task of offering a standard of life lower 'than the situation of the independent labourer of the lowest class' in order to sift the 'really destitute' from the 'impostor'. Within this provision, however, there was still a need, the Commissioners suggested, to distinguish between different types of inmate. The impotent and aged, children, able-bodied females, and able-bodied males, they argued, should ideally be housed in separate buildings 'as very different qualities both moral and intellectual are required for the management of such dissimilar classes' (Checkland 1974 : 429). But since economy was a major concern, this form of classification was not adopted in practice during the following century or so of the Poor Law's existence. Instead, where the needs of the destitute and disabled were classified separately, they were gradually met by other forms of statutory and voluntary residential care. The hospital, asylum, jail, reformatory, barrack schools, and voluntary homes for children are all examples of the alternatives which the Victorians provided for potential inmates of the workhouse.

In practice these forms of care appear to have shared much in common with the day-to-day regime of the workhouse: regular and rigid timetables; batch sleeping and eating; limited space; uniforms; monotonous and limited diet; lack of contact with the outside world. This, of course, resulted in a noticeable apathy amongst inmates, what Emma Shephard in 1863 described as 'the listless look, the dull vacuity, the lack of all interest except for the petty details of tea versus gruel – potatoes versus rice' (Longmate 1974 : 171).

In the context of the social and political concerns of Victorian welfare policy, residential care of the kind provided by the workhouse had a very wide remit:

> 'On the one hand the prevention of idleness and fraud, the main-tenance of law and order and the enforcement of family responsi-bility, on the other hand the provision of care, treatment, asylum and the last refuge. These functions were found to conflict and compete, both in the principles behind the legislation on poor relief, and in the practices of those who provided it.'
>
> (Jordan 1976 : 126)

By the time the final major review of the Poor Law took place, in the early 1900s, most inmates of the workhouse were classified as impo-tent; for the workhouse had become not only the last resort of families and individuals in trouble but also the last resort when other forms of institutional care failed. Yet both of the Royal Commission reports which were produced at this time shared a concern that the work-house should not abandon its deterrent role by providing a quality of life which would attract those still able to fend for themselves. In the words of the minority report, 'the General Mixed Workhouse, with its stigma of pauperism, its dull routine, its exaction of such work as its inmates can perform and its deterrent regulations seems a fitting place in which to end a misspent life' (Townsend 1964 : 25).

It was the change in the legal and administrative base of statutory residential care heralded by the 'death' of the Poor Law in post-war Britain, which marked the beginning of the growth of social work involvement in this area. Local authority departments with responsi-bility for specific client groups began to establish residential re-sources, particularly for children and elderly people, whose declared function was to meet client need. This core of provision has been added to since, and amalgamated under the residential sector of the local authority social service departments which emerged from the 1970 legislation.

But legislative and administrative change does not seem to have laid the ghost of the deterrent residential provision of three and a half centuries. It seems to have lived on, not just in the use of buildings, but also in the attitudes of the public and the professionals to residential care.

In 1975 the Personal Social Services Council (PSSC) report *Living and Working in Residential Homes* commented:

'in order to understand the reluctance and fear which some people feel to the prospect of being "put away" . . . it is necessary to recognise how much influence the deterrent principles, stigmatisation, and punitive aspects of previous public services still have on personal attitudes despite the very different nature and purpose of residential care today.'   (PSSC 1975 : 7)

In 1977 the president of the Residential Care Association stressed the need 'to erase . . . the image of the home for the elderly as the old workhouse, homes and hostels for the mentally ill and the mentally handicapped as the old madhouse, and children's community homes as old reform schools' (RCA 1977 : 12).

The image conveyed here is one in which residential social workers have to battle with a number of deeply rooted ideas and irrational fears, in order to establish the true identity of their new approach to residential care. It is a battle which is in many ways unique to the field of residential social work. For whilst the language and practice of casework, community work, and groupwork can be seen to have altered with time, there is still a 'core' to these methods which can be traced through the history of social work. It is more difficult to identify a 'core' to residential social work. Residential care has served a multitude of functions and has been provided by many occupational groups and private individuals. As the last resort for people unable to live in the community it is a form of welfare provision which has reflected changes in attitude to society's casualties. In the view of the Williams Committee: 'at any period of time, the residential establishment reflects what the community wants for those in need and therefore what kind of care the staff are expected to give them. Changes in social philosophy very directly affect the job the staff are called on to do.' (Williams 1967 : 36).

So, even though the development of the forms of residential care can be traced, it is difficult to find much continuity between the duties and tasks of, say, a workhouse master and those of a head of a community home, elderly persons' home, or hostel for the mentally disordered.

In order, then, to establish the identity of residential social work it is important to determine what residential social workers are taking on in their battle with a past, in which they have played so little part, and exactly what new dimension they are expected to bring to residential care.

The potential of residential social work

This is not a subject which has attracted a great deal of attention in the literature. Over the last ten years or so a number of implicit assumptions have been made about the social work potential of a variety of residential solutions but these have not been subjected, as yet, to any rigorous scrutiny. Instead, commentators and practitioners have largely drifted into one of three camps. Either they are generally optimistic about the potential of residential care for engineering individual change and well-being; or they are fundamentally pessimistic, doubting that any benefits can be derived by individuals who become involved in this form of intervention; or (and this is very much a minority position) they are adopting a radical stance arguing that, although there is little in current practice about which to be optimistic, residential care does have an untried potential for providing positive and alternative forms of communal living for individuals.

THE OPTIMISTS

This view has tended to dominate the various professional and policy documents which have focused on resdental care in the post-war period. (Williams 1967; CCETSW 1973; PSSC 1975). It underlies the arguments of those who wish to see residential work merging with social work.

Optimists see the development of residential care as being the gradual recognition of, and response to, a variety of human needs. The all-purpose provision of the workhouse, which met the need for housing, financial support, medical care, protection, and control, gave way in the twentieth century to a more selective and specialized range of residential provision. This range was based on the classification of inmates into groups with common personal and social needs who required different residential regimes. These regimes have become increasingly sensitive and flexible, with the aim of promoting the worth of dignity of each individual, and recognizing that individual's right to the maximum development of potential throughout his or her life. This transforms the residential solution from one of mass control and custody to one of individualized care and treatment.

The reasons why this transformation has occurred are traced to two processes: first, a general change in the climate of opinion towards society's casualties, a change which is part of the development of the British welfare system as a whole during the twentieth century; second, the growth which has taken place in knowledge about the human condition, in particular the psychological and social components of human behaviour and their influence on the organization and operation of residential institutions.

As far as the first factor is concerned, the optimists point out that residential care stemmed from two primary 'impulses' – on the one hand, a need to protect society from the deviant and, on the other, a sense of duty towards protecting the unfortunate. While state provision in the nineteenth century stressed the first, it also took on the task of the second, and the conflict between the two became increasingly apparent as the century progressed. This conflict resulted in a separation of these functions by means of specialist state provision – hospitals, asylums, barrack schools, and cottage homes, as well as private and voluntary provision concerned with particular client groups.

As the state took on increasing responsibility for the welfare of the individual, new forms of assistance such as old age pensions, unemployment and sickness insurance, began to supplement the workhouse response to destitution. The result was a gradual change in the tasks which this type of residential care performed.

Optimists see the turning point as the post-war legislation which gave local government departments a variety of responsibilities to provide residential care for those in need of support or protection, on principles as far removed as possible from the spirit of the Poor Law. The result was the use of both statutory and voluntary provision on a small, homely scale, which became increasingly sensitive to differences as well as similarities in the conditions of children, adolescents, the elderly, the physically handicapped, and the mentally disordered.

When these kinds of statutory residential provision became a part of the same local authority departments' responsibility in 1971 it became possible to view them, along with their voluntary counterparts, as part of a spectrum of resources available to help those in need: 'one therapeutic resource in a wide range of possibilities' (Brearley 1977 : 60) which social workers could draw on; a resource which, in order to fulfil its potential, needed to be informed by the same basic values and concerns as other social work strategies.

This shift in attitude is also evident in the penal and health services. In both, the post-war period brought a questioning of the value of custodial care and an emphasis on trying to meet the needs of such groups as offenders, the mentally disordered, and the physically handicapped, without resorting to residential solutions. What is more, where residential care in hostels is used for such groups there has been an increased insistence that it should be used to motivate and rehabilitate residents so that they are helped to return to the community as quickly as possible. With this shift in approach has come a recognition that such residential tasks belong more appropriately to social workers than to prison or hospital staff.

As for the second factor, the growth of the social sciences brought with it a number of studies of residential care, its dynamics and effects. Goffman's account of 'total institutions' in general and psychiatric institutions in particular (Goffman 1961) is cited as having key importance in identifying the major characteristics of residential care and in promoting a more questioning attitude to its use. At the same time, a number of British studies in the 1960s and early 1970s described some of the major forms of residential care for various client groups. Townsend's *The Last Refuge* looked at residential care provided for the elderly (Townsend 1964); Meacher's *Taken for a Ride* (Meacher 1972) documented the development of separatist provision for the elderly mentally ill; Morris in *Put Away* (Morris 1969) surveyed hospital care for the mentally handicapped; both King and his colleagues (King, Raynes, and Tizard 1971) and Oswin (1973) looked at the residential care provided for handicapped children.

What emerged from all these studies were accounts of areas of residential care which still stripped individuals of their previous identities and 'warehoused' them, often in drab, routinized environments. Such studies fed discussions about abandoning the residential solution for a range of client groups – or at least abandoning those residential solutions which were long-term and large-scale. They also fed the concern of practitioners (particularly in establishments for children and large psychiatric hospitals) to develop ways of caring which, rather than 'institutionalizing' or 'stunting' individuals, helped them grow and develop their potential.

The therapeutic community, an approach developed in some large psychiatric institutions, was probably the most sophisticated result of this concern and it was adopted in a small number of residential establishments (Hinshelwood and Manning 1979; Jansen 1980).

Alongside this growth in the social sciences came new developments in medical knowledge – both technological and pharmaceutical – which began to reduce the necessity of long-term medical care for the physically and mentally disabled. As a result, the contribution which medicine could make to the care of such groups as the mentally handicapped and elderly became more clearly differentiated from their ongoing social care, and the relevance of a social work approach to residential provision emerged.

In sum, then, optimists suggest that the development of residential care over the last 140 years can be seen as an evolution which has culminated in the recent and 'natural' move of residential care into the realm of social work; 'natural' because, as the importance of the individual emerged, then a social work approach to his or her residential provision was seen as the most appropriate response.

In surveying the field of residential social work, however, the optimists have to acknowledge that there is a long way to go before the individualized approach to caring which characterizes the final stage of the evolution is realized. Difficulties in recruiting and retaining staff continue; scandals and inquiries punctuate the scene; and residential care continues to be seen as 'second best' for both residents and staff.

The answer to this, optimists argue, is to raise the status of residential social work in two ways. First, by establishing comprehensive training in this field so that it is seen on a par with field social work. In 1967 the Williams Committee suggested this could be achieved by establishing residential social work as a separate profession with its own training. By the mid-seventies, however, the proposal was adopted of establishing a training for residential social work which was on the same pattern as that available to fieldworkers. Whether this will lead to an increase in the number of qualified people returning to residential work is as yet unclear. If it does, then it will, in the view of the optimists, take the evolution of residential care a stage further.

The second ingredient vital to this evolution is, the optimists suggest, clarification of the principles and practices which will promote a social work approach to residential care; a framework for care within which objectives are established and used to inform exchanges between staff and residents. When staff are sure of their task and residents and relatives of their rights, then the experience of this form of care will be enhanced and its standing in the eyes of the community increased.

For the optimists, the realization of the full potential of residential social work is dependent upon an increase in the training of residential workers and a clarification of the functions of residential care.

THE PESSIMISTS

Although the pessimists' position has not been promoted in the same way as that of the optimists, it has emerged strongly from a number of studies of institutional life and it underlies much negative professional and lay reaction to the use of residential care.

Pessimists challenge the notion that it is possible to view residential care as gradually evolving in a positive direction. For them the outstanding characteristic of residential provision has been its relatively static state; its inability to change is seen as a persistent feature of its history.

For the pessimists, residential care has always been regarded as 'a second best' provision by the public at large and this image reflects on both residents and staff. As a result, there have always been difficulties in recruiting and keeping staff, as well as in attempting to change care practices. The reason for the low status of this field is, they suggest, rooted in the nature of British society. Thus they are pessimistic about the chances of social work bringing about a fundamental change in approach to caring in this field.

Miller in her analysis of residential care suggests that residential institutions and groups within them should be seen as part of 'a dynamic social system with emotional and ideological burdens to shoulder as well as the more obvious but less difficult tasks of rehabilitation and cure' (Miller 1974 : 265). An examination of these burdens and their effects is the key, in her view, to increasing our understanding of residential social work.

As far as the 'ideological burden' is concerned, Miller points out that what residential care does, and has always done, is to provide shelter or care when there is a temporary or permanent breakdown in the basic source of care – the family. Those finding themselves 'in care' today are, as were their nineteenth-century counterparts, not necessarily more dependent or disabled than others sharing their condition. What they do lack is appropriate care by family or friendship networks. The result of this is that moving from the community into residential care is a public declaration not only of a lack of support but also of a more general lack of social standing. Miller and Gwynne in their study of residential establishments for the young physically handicapped and chronic sick found that when entering care residents experienced a double rejection.

> 'They have for the most part been rejected as individuals, in that their families are no longer willing or able to look after them. More importantly, by crossing the boundary into the institution, whether voluntarily or not, they fall into a rejected category of non-contributors to and non-participants in society, and indeed are virtually non-members of society.'
>
> (Miller and Gwynne 1972 : 73)

An analogy with the nineteenth-century paupers, whose entry into the workhouse stripped them of citizens' rights, does not seem difficult to make. In a society which still places so much store on the work ethic, crossing the boundary into an institution is still a public acknowledgement of failure and worthlessness.

What is more, the priorities established within the residential care field also reflect this 'work-achievement' ideology. The history of residential care clearly shows a pattern of differential provision between client groups. Children have fared best. In nineteenth-century terms they were seen as most 'saveable' and both statutory and voluntary efforts were made to provide them with separate care. During the twentieth century there has continued to be a relatively richer range of residential resources for them compared with other client groups. At the other end of the scale residential resources for the elderly have been of a more limited nature (Townsend 1964).

The pessimists suggest that this differential treatment is not just the

result of humanitarian concerns – the 'appeal' of the child as opposed
to that of the elderly or permanently disabled – rather, it reflects the
differential importance attached to those in our society who are
capable of filling a productive role. For the pessimists it is the dominant ideas, or ideology, of our society which set particular burdens or
constraints on the nature of residential care.

From this analysis a view emerges which directly challenges that of
the optimists. The pessimists do not see residential social workers as
being engaged in a battle with ideas from the past, about the stigma of
residential care. Instead, they see stigma as a continuing part of
residential provision, drawing its sustenance from ideas rooted in
society today. Within the pessimists' camp a differential emphasis is
placed on the importance of psychological and social factors in sustaining the stigma inherent in residential care.

Miller emphasizes the contribution made by psychological factors:

> 'generally speaking the "old", the "bad", the "stupid" and the
> "mad" tend to fare rather badly. These groups represent extremes
> of the human condition which are often difficult or disturbing to
> face since they evoke anxieties in us all about our own mortality,
> guilt, incompetence and irrationality . . . the areas of most pain and
> need which remain unprovided for in terms of interest and money
> tell us a great deal about the true range of our care and concern and
> identify those problems which are beyond the range of our emo-
> tional and financial investment.'   (Miller 1974 : 261)

If this is accepted, then it would appear that the scandals, inquiries,
lack of staff, lack of training, poor facilities, and routinized care
practices, which have been constant features of residential care are
not just a matter of past policies and philosophies but are a reflection
of the current commitment to groups who are in need of residential
support. The limits of this commitment, Miller suggests, are set by
the deeply seated emotional responses which we all share towards
those who find themselves in residential care. As 'rejects' they remind
us of our own vulnerability and the investment we are prepared
to make in their care reflects a deep ambivalence of attitude to
them.

At an interpersonal level, Miller and Gwynne in their study of
institutions for the physically handicapped and Menzies in her study
of nursing care (Miller and Gwynne 1972; Menzies 1960), suggest

that this 'emotional burden' which residential staff take on has very real implications for the way they relate to residents.

Menzies argues (in relation to nursing) that staff 'are confronted with the threat and reality of suffering and death as few lay people are'. As a result, the tasks they are required to carry out can evoke powerful emotional responses towards patients ranging from fear and disgust to affection and sexual excitement. In order to protect staff from the emotional impact of these experiences, the nursing service has evolved an approach to caring which structures and controls interaction between the nurse and patient. Central to this approach is splitting up staff contact with patients by breaking down the workload of a ward and department into 'lists of tasks each of which is allocated to a particular nurse'. As a consequence, the chances of nurses developing an intense personal relationship with any one patient in their care is decreased and patients experience a variety of nurses performing different services for them – often unrelated to their idiosyncratic needs. As an approach to caring it succeeds in deflecting anxieties from interpersonal interaction (the prime task) to ritual, routine, and procedure (secondary tasks). However, in doing so it produces 'a kind of depersonalization and elimination of individual distinctiveness in both nurse and patient.'

Menzies describes this approach as a 'defence mechanism against anxiety' and Miller and Gwynne develop this notion further in their study of residental units for physically handicapped adults by suggesting that the primary models of care which have emerged in these establishments are the result of the defences staff have adopted in carrying out their primary task.

This analysis of the dynamics of residential care challenges the view that a spread in the values and skills of social work among residential staff is sufficient in itself to change residential care into residential social work.

What the pessimists point out is that any change will be mediated through the wider social and emotional context of residential care, and that this context sets limits on what can be achieved by residential strategies. In clarifying the aims and objectives of residential care and spelling out more clearly the residential task, it is not sufficient to focus solely on the dynamics within institutions. Account has to be taken of the way in which the dominant ideas about human worth and emotional responses to disability and deprivation, influence the theory and practice of residential care.

They point out, too, that the stigma associated with residential care cannot be dismissed as a 'hangover' from a past era. It is part of our current attitudes to individual worth and as such plays an important part in shaping the ideas and work of those in the residential field.

The lesson here for residential social work seems to be that it is not possible to assume that the adoption of objectives which emphasize the provision of opportunities for growth, maturation, and independence, will necessarily transform the field of residential care or extend choice for client groups.

In addition to this emphasis on psychological and interpersonal factors, some of the pessimists have focused on the social and economic base of the mandate which residential care has been given. Their concern has been to analyse the nature of welfare provision and the nature of social work in industrial capitalist society. Where residential social work is referred to, it is seen as part of a wider process – an example of the way in which particular trends in welfare and social work are working their way through an area of provision.

To this group of pessimists, social services reflect, in their levels of provision and their criteria of allocation, the balance of power and the quality of the relationship between deprived and privileged groups at any one point in time. As part of that provision, residential care reflects the basic economic inequalities and conflicts which are part of industrial capitalism. As Holman and Schorr amongst others have pointed out (Holman 1980; Schorr 1975), state residential provision for children is not used by families from all social classes; it is children from the lowest social classes who find themselves in local authority or voluntary community homes. They claim that there is no evidence to suggest that this is because rejection or neglect is more rife amongst lower-class parents than their middle- or upper-class counterparts. Rather than reflecting a response to individual difficulties of this kind, residential provision reflects a response to social and economic inequality. It is part of a society in which wealthier families needing alternative forms of care for their children purchase it, whilst poorer parents are dependent on public provision. What is more, the privately purchased alternatives do not share the social stigma attached to residential care alternatives for the family. When parents choose to delegate the upbringing of their children to nursemaids and private boarding school education they are viewed as giving them 'the best start in life'.

This analysis suggests that the low status of residential care is not just a reflection of the fact that it is 'second best' to family care. Low status, poor resources, and stigma are attached to certain forms of residential care – care which is publicly provided and which, in an economic system equating income with autonomy, is seen as inferior to both family care and privately purchased alternatives.

This is part of a pattern which is not unique to residential work with children. Residential social workers, together with their fieldwork colleagues, work mainly with those individuals and families 'in need' at the lower end of the social scale. In doing so they inevitably provide a solution to the problems of daily living which, Jordan argues, is shaped by the same ideology which created the nineteenth-century workhouse (Jordan 1974); an ideology which stresses the worth and dignity of those individuals able to provide for themselves and stigmatizes those who have to turn to the state for support. It follows that changes in the form of residential provision over time have not been expressions of a change of approach to society's casualties. They reflect compromises reached in the class conflict which lies at the heart of capitalist society.

In 1948 when the 'death of the Poor Law' was announced with the passing of the National Assistance Act the vision of future residential provision for the elderly was one in which workhouses would be replaced by small home-like establishments where 'the old master and inmate relationship [would be] replaced by one more nearly approaching that of a hotel manager and his guests' (Townsend 1964 : 32).

The implicit suggestion here, the pessimists argue, is that the best guarantee of individualized care and the maintenance of dignity, is a situation in which care is given as a service in exchange for money. It follows that the best that publicly provided residential care can aspire to is necessarily limited because those it caters for cannot engage in this kind of exchange. They are dependent groups in terms of both their individual needs and their lack of purchasing power and as such remain a constant source of threat to the autonomy of those who are self-supporting. Operating in this context residential care, like other welfare responses, will inevitably be performing deterrent as well as caring and controlling functions.

The importance that the optimists attach to the influence of a social work approach in changing the traditions of residential care, disappears in the face of this analysis. For social work practice and values cannot be separated from the wider social and economic context in which they operate. As the 'social conscience' of an unequal society social workers are unable to promote the growth, change, and individual choice which their language suggests.

It follows, too, that the type of interaction developed in establishments between workers and residents is as much a reflection of political and moral stances to the dependent as it is of the primitive emotional responses which the psychological pessimists describe. Similarly, the status of residential care staff, their isolation and power in relation to colleagues and residents, has a wider social and economic base.

This view, then, suggests that there are further constraints on the potential of residential strategies in social work, but not constraints wholly unique to the residential situation. The pessimists place the problems faced by residential social workers in the more general context of problems faced by social workers operating in capitalist society. If there is a uniqueness, it may lie in the fact that as a welfare response and a social work strategy, residential care is very visible and therefore its practice may show very sharply the deep contradictions which lie at the heart of a capitalist welfare system.

THE RADICALS

A radical position on the potential of residential social work has only recently emerged in the literature and it presents several important challenges to the ideas which have been more fully developed in the optimist and pessimist camps (Brake and Bailey 1980 : 86).

Essentially the radicals, like some of the pessimists, locate residential care in its social and economic context. For the radicals, state residential solutions are a highly stigmatized form of welfare, catering primarily for groups who are socially and economically deprived. The low status and poor standards of residential provision reflect the inequality inherent in the structure of British society. Residential care buttresses the status quo.

Where the radicals diverge from the pessimists is over the issue of the family. The radicals question the assumption made by the pessimists that residential care is inherently inferior to life in the nuclear family or the community. The radicals point out that there is ample evidence that these living arrangements too can become intolerable for individuals. In the face of this, they argue that state residential care needs to be seen as having a potential for offering a positive option, 'a possible forum for the development of reasonable alternatives which would point the way to new forms of creative, collective living' (Brake and Bailey 1980 : 105).

While radicals do not accept the optimists' view that there has been a gradual and general improvement in current residential provision, they are loathe to accept the pessimists' view that 'present shortcomings are necessarily permanent'. Instead, they maintain that there exist opportunities within the current system to create the kind of residential solutions which do more than merely reflect the dominant concerns of the present political order.

The key problem they identify as facing those who attempt to work with these opportunities, is that of avoiding the creation of residential communities which are divorced from the world outside the unit. Lee and Pithers, looking at the radical possibilities of residential child care, maintain that the potential exists for 'providing alternative experiences which challenge the immutability of present social forms but which at the same time do not run away from the reality the child will have to face' (Brake and Bailey 1980 : 112). They suggest that the realization of this potential is dependent on residential workers and others striving for a number of changes in the current service. The changes which they list include one which the optimists argue is essential to achieving a new approach to residential care – the recognition that residential work is social work and that it requires an increase in professional training. As radicals, Lee and Pithers add to this a number of other changes: the unionization of residential workers to improve their conditions of service; the conscientization of residential workers through increased contact and exchange of common problems; resistance to closures of residential establishments; resistance to the stigmatization of residential care; and the imposition of minimum standards in residential units. In other words, it is on the basis of an overall campaign to improve status and standards in residential care that the development of its potential is seen as taking place.

What the radical camp offers is a way of locating the current problems faced in residential work in their social context. At the same time the radicals indicate that it is possible to develop practice which tackles some of these problems through the creation of viable alternative forms of communal living. It combines elements from the optimist and pessimist camps, and suggests specific ways in which residential staff can influence the constraints within which they are working. In taking this position, the radicals highlight an important question for residential workers to consider. Just how far are the functions of state residential care determined by the wider welfare ideology? Their analysis suggests that, whilst there are several persistent social, philosophical, and political factors which have shaped the residential care system in Britain, it is still possible for residential workers to use that system in a radically different way.

Summary

In this chapter I have begun to explore some of the key issues which are raised by an examination of residential social work. I have suggested that as the connection between social work and residential care is a relatively recent one, there are still considerable difficulties in drawing boundaries around that sector of residential care which falls into the territory of residential social work. These difficulties arise from the continuing debates and uncertainties surrounding such issues as professional identity and training, as well as the lack of any administrative unity across the territory.

I have suggested that two areas important to developing an understanding of the nature of residential social work are first, its heritage and, second, the views currently held about its potential as a form of social intervention. In tracing its heritage one becomes aware of the diverse expectations which have been and continue to be placed on it. These add to the uncertainties with which many residential workers find themselves negotiating. In considering the current views, one becomes aware again of diversity. On the one hand, the optimists point to the gradual improvement in residential care which will ultimately be secured as its links to social work strengthen; on the other hand, the pessimists point to its persistent and inevitable failure to provide positive experiences; while the newly emerging radicals fuse elements of both by suggesting that residential solutions have not only a potential for care but also challenge our accepted notions of family and community life.

2

Residential care and family care

There are over 200,000 individuals currently living in the care of residential workers (CSO 1978). Each of them has entered into this particular living arrangement as a result of a unique combination of social and family circumstances; individual incapacities and behaviours; and the availability of residential and other forms of welfare provision. Although these individuals come from some of the most disabled and disadvantaged groups in British society they do not, by any means, represent the most extreme conditions which exist within those groups. Thousands more, with greater personal and social difficulties, live alone, or with friends and family, in the community.

The reason for this is that welfare policies in Britain have always been based on the assumption that the prime responsibility for the care of dependants and incapacitated individuals lies with their natural families. Policies of all kinds have encouraged the view that recognition of this responsibility is a 'normal' or 'natural' part of family life (Land and Parker 1978). As a result, state residential provision has always been seen as a last resort and has played a very residual part in the care of deviant, dependent, and disabled groups. Indeed, as economic restraint becomes an increasingly important influence on the development of welfare provision in Britain, it is likely that this residual role will shrink even further.

As a provision of last resort, residential care is usually only made available by the state to the individual when his 'natural' care and support systems have failed in some way. Acceptance of this provision in effect removes the prime responsibility for care and control from the private sphere of family life to the public sphere of welfare and social work services. In a society concerned to uphold the notion that the privacy of family life is all-important, this visible intrusion, and transfer of family responsibility, raises a number of dilemmas both for those providing residential establishments and for those working and living in them. Some of these dilemmas have already been identified in the discussion of the potential of residential social work contained in chapter one.

For the optimists, residential care can be a positive response to situations in which the family is no longer able or willing to provide care for one of its members. It can offer a refuge from, or substitute for, family life. Indeed, for some, it can offer opportunities which were never part of their own family situation. The problem the optimists face lies in realizing this positive potential. The dilemma is how to replace traditional, custodial care, organized around the needs of an institution, with care centred on the needs of individual residents.

For the pessimists, it is the transfer of responsibility for caring, from the family to the residential unit, that raises problems. In their view, it is this transfer which generates the stigma attached to residential care. The pessimists argue that once the family hands over its caring responsibilities, the individual concerned is 'cast out' of society and placed in a world which can never be more than 'second best'; a world in which the shame of social rejection shapes the relationships between staff and residents. In addition, some think that the dilemmas raised by this transfer of responsibility for caring are increased because the majority of families who do relinquish their responsibilities are drawn from particular sections of society. They are families whose lack of resources leave them little choice in determining how to care for dependent or incapacitated members, and the stigma they incur in using state provision adds to the general underprivilege they experience in their family circumstances.

The radicals, like the pessimists, focus on the stigma which is attached to the transfer of caring responsibilities. They argue that the source of this stigma is an unquestioning acceptance that life in a residential community is bound to be inferior to life in a family. For the radicals it is this belief in the inferiority of residential care that raises dilemmas for residential workers and residents. In their view, residential care can offer – for some – a preferable alternative to family and community living. They stress the need for residential workers to challenge the stigma attached to their units and to work for an acceptance that periods spent in residential care can be a helpful experience for individuals.

The relationship, then, between the family and residential care is a relationship riddled with contradictions. This is because residential solutions not only can remove prime responsibility for caring from the private sphere of family life to the public sphere of welfare and social work, but can also be a complete substitute for family life. In a society which stresses that the individual and the family should take prime responsibility for welfare, such provision must pose a threat, as well as offering a source of relief. What is more, the power to determine who should be offered this form of provision has fallen increasingly to social workers – a professional group which claims that a major part of its activities is focused on 'supporting' and 'strengthening' the family.

In this chapter I want to trace some of these contradictions by looking at two of the main issues in the complex debate about the family and residential care. I believe that before beginning to develop theory and practice in residential work, it is of great importance to look at the ways in which notions of the family have been used in discussions about residential care. For such discussions bring out the constraints that are placed on both the provision of residential solutions and the development of particular forms of residential care and practice. It is with this in mind that I discuss first, the views held about the relationship between family responsibility and the provision of residential care and, second, the ways in which notions of 'normal' family life have influenced the development of particular forms of residential practice.

Family responsibility and residential provision

It is possible to trace a concern with reinforcing the family's responsibility for caring for its dependent and incapacitated members through almost four centuries of social legislation. From 1598 when it was spelt out in statute that, 'it shall be the duty of the father, grandfather, grandmother, husband or child of a poor, old, blind, lame or impotent person . . . if possessed of sufficient means, to relieve or maintain that person', the expectation of the state has been that it is the family who should care for its dependants – whether the condition of dependency is a natural consequence of age or a consequence of disability, illness or deviance (Bruce 1961 : 34).

The provision of a public care system, to be used if families failed to perform such duties, was a far from simple matter. Its very existence was seen by some as undermining the 'natural' networks of family support. In their review of the Poor Law in the early 1830s the Royal Commissioners noted that, 'the duty of supporting parents and children in old age or infirmity, is so strongly enforced by our natural feelings that it is often well performed even among savages and almost always so in a nation deserving the name of civilisation' (Checkland 1974 : 115). But they went on to argue that there was evidence to suggest that in England this duty was being increasingly neglected. In their view, Poor Law residential care was being used as a way out of this obligation and, in order to stop this sad state of affairs, the Commissioners suggested that residential provision should be made which positively strengthened the resolve of families to retain their responsibilities. Deterrent workhouse regimes were therefore promoted as a major means of reinforcing the notion of family responsibility in nineteenth-century England.

The consequences of this development have already been touched on. As workhouse populations grew increasingly infirm, voluntary groups and individuals involved in inspecting and visiting, began to publicize the fact that workhouses were an inappropriate response to inmates' needs. The physically sick and mentally disordered were identified as requiring the kind of specialist treatment which could only be provided under non-deterrent conditions. Children, however, were seen as having a greater chance of becoming disciplined and contributing members of society if they could be separated from the contaminating influence of the population of the general workhouse. In this vein, the argument was developed that less deterrent residential provision should be provided for elderly or handicapped adults whose life styles had been such that they deserved more than workhouse care. They were the 'deserving' whose destitution or dependence was no fault of their own.

These arguments were, of course, countered by those who believed as the Commissioners had, that the provision of a less deterrent form of state care would encourage families to 'give up' caring for their dependants, and would sap the drive towards independence and self reliance so vital to the healthy growth of a capitalist society. As a consequence, the development of residential care based on less deterrent principles was slow.

The debates which shaped residential provision in the nineteenth and early twentieth centuries did not just revolve around the issue of reinforcing the family's natural responsibilities. Those directly concerned with arguing for residential alternatives to general workhouse or prison care were quick to point out that the problem was a complicated one. In their view, the behaviour of some individuals clearly indicated that certain families were not capable of providing the right kind of care and control for their members. They were not 'normal', 'healthy', or 'respectable' families and, if they were not relieved of their 'natural' responsibilities, then the consequences could threaten the structure of society. If they were to be relieved, then it was through residential provision based on sound moral principles that the threat of disorder could be tackled.

It was this outlook which informed the work of some of the pioneers in child care. Mary Carpenter, Dr Barnado, and others stressed, time and again, that the right kind of residential provision for deprived and delinquent children could save them from moral degeneracy and, at the same time, could save society from the consequences of their activities (Carlebach 1970).

There was also a slowly growing acceptance that the family could not always make adequate provision for other groups too. The arguments for increasing asylum provision for the mentally ill and mentally handicapped were often justified on the grounds that family or community care for such groups was a rather unsatisfactory expedient. What was needed was specialist treatment in isolated residential communities which would provide more effective care than the family and would also ensure that those with such conditions did not establish families of their own. The ideas of the eugenics movement in the early twentieth century clearly suggested that there were categories of people for whom family life was not acceptable in any form. As a consequence, certain families gained permission to relinquish their responsibilities to the 'experts'.

Nigel Middleton's study of residential child care during the first half of the twentieth century provides a vivid picture of the practical consequences which these debates on family responsibility had for one group within the community (Middleton 1971). The slow growth of Poor Law and voluntary child care establishments, together with the introduction of new forms of residential care after the First World War for families who had lost their breadwinner in action, resulted in an increased range of responses to destitute and delinquent children. Within this provision, the predominant notion that residential care should remain deterrent and should only be made available to families following a public declaration of failure, coexisted with the notion that some families should be compensated for their inability to provide adequate care for their dependants. The result, Middleton suggests, was differential provision for different social groups within a system where care practices still reflected a Poor Law approach.

The contradictory views held about the relationship of family responsibility to residential provision were brought sharply to the surface during the economic difficulties experienced in Britain during the 1920s and 1930s. As families were increasingly exhorted to maintain all their members with the minimum of state help the deterrent nature of public residential care was re-emphasized. The result was that, in some parts of the country, there was a growing reluctance to relieve families of their caring responsibilities by providing a roof over the head for some of their dependants. Yet, at the same time, attempts were made by government to deal with unemployed adolescents by removing them from home and sending them to training hostels in other parts of the country (Wilson 1977 : 125). Faced with family resistance to this move, the Ministry of Labour found itself trying to convince the public that it was 'fit and proper' for some families to relinquish their responsibilities for this particular group of dependants.

The Second World War brought new perspectives on the issue of family responsibility and residential provision. Policies to provide sufficient accommodation to meet the medical needs of a nation at war resulted in the 'opening up' of a number of residential communities. As a result, particular groups, such as the mentally disordered, found themselves a low priority as far as residential provision was concerned and their families were expected once more to take the prime responsibility of caring. This was not, however, the experience of all dependent groups. The nation's need for female labour during wartime resulted in increased state provision being offered to relieve mothers of some of their child care responsibilities (Wilson 1977).

It was shifts such as these, in the use of residential provision of all kinds, that led to a questioning of some of the previous assumptions held about the nature and use of residential provision. This questioning was sharpened by concern about the quality of life being offered in some of the residential communities which had been 'opened' for wider use. The drab, poverty-stricken existence of some groups of residents in both Poor Law and voluntary establishments became more visible to the public at large than at any period before.

What is fascinating about this period is that at the same time as the question of the quality of residential care was opened to public debate, so was the question of the quality of care provided by certain families. The poor physical condition of children evacuated from large industrial towns together with what seemed to be their limited experience of 'normal' family life became a hotly debated subject in the press. As the war continued 'unbilletable' mothers and children were identified as a group needing help of a special kind – tightly supervised residential provision which would ensure their 'moral rehabilitation'. In other words, residential care came to be seen not just as a means of 'saving' children from inadequate families and mothers, but as a solution to the problem of inadequacy itself.

In this climate it is not surprising that the period which immediately followed the war was one in which the issue of residential care and family responsibility came to the fore.

Attention was given to considering the existing organization of residential care for a variety of groups and to recommending changes. In 1946 residential care for children was subject to the scrutiny of the Curtis Committee whose report led to the creation of local authority children's departments. The Committee's detailed descriptions of the residential child care provision visited convey the continuing taint of deterrent regimes concerned with control, discipline, and uniformity. It recommended a complete transformation of the state's approach to caring for children. These recommendations were carried out by the Children's Act of 1948.

In the same year the National Assistance Act separated local authority residential provision for the elderly and handicapped from financial assistance to those groups. The Poor Law was declared dead and with it the bleak, drab, uniform regimes of the workhouse.

Experience of caring for the mentally disordered during a period when asylum care was a scarce resource had also suggested that the newly created local authority mental welfare departments had a role to play in supervising care within the family. Although a decade or more was to pass before 'community care' became accepted policy in this field, the seeds of the idea had been sown.

These changes in the organization of sectors of residential care reflected changes which had taken place in the notion of family responsibility.

Post-war concerns with the reconstruction and re-establishment of family life, took up issues of the quality of emotional as well as physical care within the family. In 1948 the sub-committee of the Women's Group on Public Welfare issued a report, *The Neglected Child and his Family* (1948) which conveys this emphasis of the debate particularly well. The sub-committee endeavoured: 'to explore and chart the field with regard to children for whose physical, mental and spiritual welfare the community must concern itself owing to the inadequacy of their parents' care' (Women's Group 1948 : iv).

The report identified the existence of what appeared to be an increasing number of 'substandard' or 'problem' families who were failing not only to provide adequate material care for their offspring but also adequate emotional care. The failure of these families, the group argued, could not be remedied by removing children from their parents and receiving them into institutional or foster parent care; for, 'it is difficult to find a substitute for the feelings of security provided by one's own family circle', however inadequate. Removing family responsibility in this way would be an 'easy answer' and 'psychologically unsound'. The alternative was to provide 'a setting . . . wherein parents can build a satisfactory home life for their children. For the care of children remains an intensely personal relationship. Society can provide a favourable environment only, it will always remain with the individual to create a home within it' (Women's Group 1948 : 123).

The report went on to suggest that such settings could be promoted by social work intervention in various forms, ranging from intensive home visiting to residential situations which whole families would enter in order to be rehabilitated.

In other words, family life, however inadequate, was seen as providing an emotional climate vital to individual growth and development. It was a climate which could not be replicated in alternative forms of care and it was because of this that the family had to be helped to maintain its responsibility for caring. To abandon this responsibility could only damage the mental health of all concerned and, whilst initially this argument focused on the care of children, it was to be increasingly used in the next two decades in relation to other dependent groups.

Concern about the kind of institutional care being offered to the elderly, mentally disordered, physically handicapped, and adolescent and adult offenders led to an increased questioning of the merits of residential care and discussion and gradual experimentation with non-residential alternatives. Evidence was produced to show that residential care could be a damaging and inappropriate way of meeting a range of individual needs, and family care (or more nebulously 'community care') was promoted as a more 'stimulating' and 'individualized' alternative for disabled and deprived groups. A family or community setting, it was argued, offered opportunities and an emotionally secure base from which the individual could build a more independent life style as a member of a normal community. As such it was promoted as being obviously better, if available, than the specialist institutional care which had previously been developed for such groups.

In the post-war period, then, the notion of family responsibility has had its nineteenth-century base strengthened. For family care is seen now not just as the most 'natural' way in which an individual's needs are met in the material sense, but also as the repository of all that is good in the emotional sense. The consequences of this view has been to imply that removing an individual from his family situation can only be depriving and damaging and that residential care needs to be considered as a last resort. Most of the key social policy statements of the last thirty years reflect this view. For example, the report of the Committee on Children and Young Persons (1960) stated that:

'The state's principle duty is to assist the family in carrying out its proper functions. This should be done in the first instance by the provision of facilities such as housing, health services and education. Some families will need greater and more specialised help though the welfare services, but such help should always be directed towards building up the responsibility of parents whenever this is possible.'

While in the view of the Secretary of State for Social Services:

'The primary objective of the personal social services we can best describe as strengthening the capacity of the family to care for its members and to supply, as it were, the family's place where necessary: that is to provide as far as may be social support or if necessary a home for people who cannot look after themselves or be adequately looked after by their family.'   (Hansard 1970)

In the same vein *Better Services for the Mentally Handicapped* proposed that:

'Each handicapped person should live with his own family as long as this does not impose an undue burden on them or him and he and his family should receive full advice and support. If he has to leave home for a foster home, residential home or hospital, temporarily or permanently, links with his own family, should normally be maintained.'   (DHSS 1971)

It is interesting to compare this view of the relationship between family responsibility and residential care with those held in the nineteenth century. The nineteenth-century expectation seemed to be that families should maintain responsibility until destitution prevented them and many nineteenth-century residential solutions were designed to keep them doing just that – for fear of the alternative. When destitution struck, the residential solution available was one which destroyed the family unit. In post-war Britain it would appear that, whilst families are still expected to maintain responsibility for caring, it is acknowledged that the 'burden' can become too much. When this happens a residential solution is available which is described as part of a strategy to help the family 'cope better'.

In practice, this contrast is a limited one. Moroney, in his 1976 study of family and state care for two client groups, the elderly and mentally handicapped children, concluded that the notion promoted in the post-war era of the state supporting and enabling the family to care has not in fact been realized. He comments that 'relatively little is made available to families until they reach the breaking point, and often the only course open is placement in an institution' (Moroney 1976 : 107). The 'healthy' family continues to be seen as one which does not seek the help of extra-family institutions – it remains independent. As a consequence, families who do seek such help are seen as having failed by experts who consider family care to be the best possible care.

The onus still appears to remain with the family to declare itself 'bankrupt', emotionally if not materially, and when it does, an offer of residential care is often the only response. As long as this pattern persists it is difficult to see how residential solutions can ever drop their deterrent function. Although they may no longer be used to confirm that their consumers are (in the language of the Poor Law) 'morally worthless' they continue to be used to publicly confirm their failure to cope.

Yet this continuing role of deterrence has tended to slip from view as a problem facing those working in residential care today. Instead, the 'death of the Poor Law' and the provision of better standards of state care, appear to have re-activated, in some commentators, concern about the threat that some residential solutions pose to family life. B. Shenfield, in a discussion in the late 1950s of the new residential provision for the elderly, noted that 'smaller homes with a greater degree of privacy and more homely and attractive furnishings and with rules and regulations reduced to a minimum are more acceptable to frail elderly persons in care. They are also more acceptable to the consciences of their relatives.' She went on to predict that, as a result, an increasing number of 'respectable' elderly people were likely to apply for admission to such establishments (Shenfield 1957).

The fear expressed here, that better-quality residential care may sap family responsibility, has emerged as a feature of a number of post-war discussions across the range of client groups. Some commentators have suggested that it is possible to detect a real decline in the willingness of families to meet their responsibilities for the care of dependants; and they have linked this decline to the increased availability of better-quality residential alternatives.

There is no doubt that this is an argument that echoes the Poor Law assumption that only minimal provision should be made by state residential care, in order to deter families from relinquishing their duties. It is also an argument which dovetails with the emphasis on the benefits of family and community care. An early example of the way in which a concern to retain minimum standards can be presented as a way of maximizing individual welfare is to be found in the stance taken by the Royal Commission on the Poor Law in 1909. The Commission considered arguments for making workhouse provision for the elderly more comfortable and in rejecting them commented, 'It would be a great misfortune if the aged should be brought to prefer life in a workhouse . . . to an independent life amongst their friends and relatives'. This idea is still a very potent one in current discussions about residential care. At the centre of the post-war notion of community care is a contrast between dependent institutional relationships and the independent ones which can be maintained in the community.

The implication is that whatever changes have taken place in residential provision over the last century or so, the debate about its relationship to the family is still concerned with the threat posed to family responsibility by the existence of a state-supported alternative. This has a number of consequences for residential workers.

First, if residential care is provided in practice, if not in theory, on declaration of bankruptcy in the family or individual's living situation, it is limited as a social work strategy. It is being used in crisis situations and is offered as a last resort – a confirmation of failure. It is not being used as a flexible, therapeutic tool in a range of alternatives available to social work, to be offered positively in times of difficulty. It is not being used as a support, or enabler, for the individual or the family.

Second, if it is the prevailing opinion that good quality residential care ultimately saps family responsibility, then this will be reflected in the standards of care provided in the public welfare sector. This has enormous implications for the job residential staff are expected to do, the resources they are given, and the status they hold.

Third, the view that there has been a decline in the willingness of families to care for their dependants, is one which takes no account, amongst other factors, of the changes which have taken place in the ratio of working to non-working members of the population. These are changes which make the size of the family's many responsibilities greater than in any previous period (Moroney 1976). If this is not taken into account in the discussions about family responsibility and residential care, residential workers are likely to develop narrow and unrealistic expectations of the families from which residents come.

Finally, because ideas about family responsibility are part of a wider system of ideas (or ideology) about welfare – they influence the behaviour and attitudes of residential workers, residents, and relatives. To take one example, there is a great deal in the way residential workers talk about relatives of residents, which reflects the view that they are 'shirking their proper responsibilities'. Stories abound in all areas of residential care of families who 'could not be bothered' with dependent relatives, who 'gave up on them' and 'washed their hands of them' by 'shunting' them into a residential establishment. Indeed, some residential staff see themselves as morally superior. They are prepared to take on the caring responsibility for those who have been abandoned. As a result, strong negative feelings can develop in staff towards relatives with very real consequences in the encounters they have. They can also inform ongoing relationships with residents. Residents can be told, for example, of the 'worthlessness' of relatives, whilst relatives, trying to keep contact with residents, can feel unwelcome and awkward when visiting them.

The family and residential practice

Having looked at the unfavourable comparisons drawn in the postwar period between residential care and family care, it is interesting that Younghusband in her review of residential care from 1950–75 (Younghusband 1978) suggests that one of the analogies which has been used in trying to develop new approaches to residential provision has been that of the family. At the same time as notions of family life have been used to criticize the practice and even the existence of a great deal of residential care, the family has been looked to as a positive model on which to base programmes of daily living within residential establishments.

It has not of course been the major, or even the predominant model. Custody, punishment, re-education, and treatment have all been identified at various times as elements in residential solutions, and prisons, schools, and hospitals have been looked to as models on which to base the regimes being developed in what has become the residential social work field.

What is interesting, however, is that although the 'family model' of residential care has waxed and waned in popularity for a variety of client groups it has a long history of being referred to as a major means of developing residential care practices.

When the general workhouse was the main source of state residential provision, some of its visitors could not fail to notice the effects which its regime had on individual inmates. Members of Louise

Twining's Workhouse Visiting Society, created in 1858 in order to contain the growth of pauperism and improve the living conditions of the more vulnerable classes of inmates, expressed concern at the way in which the bleak, routine work regimes appeared to be sapping inmates of self-reliance. They saw the workhouse as reducing inmates to such a hopeless and powerless situation that it resulted in the creation of a class of people who demonstrated 'the vices of the slave, lack of self control, indifference to the value of property and absolute dependence on others.' Such people, it seemed, were not only unhappy in themselves but a threat to the wider community. Twining and her colleagues argued that much needed to be done to promote more morally and spiritually uplifting regimes. Particular concern was expressed about children, who if brought up in such circumstances, would only create a fresh generation of paupers. Yet the key to breaking through the vicious circle lay in much more than stricter discipline and moral education. Twining discovered that when children were herded together in large groups 'without family affections or any attempt at cultivating them' they appeared to lack those ingredients of character which were necessary to a disciplined, well-ordered existence' (Twining 1898 : 48).

She was not alone in noting this. Nassau Senior in her report on the effects of Pauper Schools for girls in 1874 commented:

'One of the greatest objections to the plan of bringing up girls in large schools is, that they are unable to get the cherishing care and individual attention that is of far more importance in the formation of character than anything else in the world. It is the fault of no one in particular that at a large school a girl's affections are not called out. The officers have so much routine work to go through, that it is absolutely impossible for them to give sufficient time to individualising and influencing the girls under their care. The inquiries I have made on all sides have convinced me that what is wanted in the education of girls is more mothering.'

(Twining 1898 : 16)

Mrs Senior did not leave it at that, but went on to describe the worth of grouping pauper children in family-type units in order to enhance the possibilities of individual influence.

Such views reflected the experiences of a number of the nineteenth-century pioneers who concerned themselves with destitute and deprived children. In their efforts to rescue such children from the dangers and immorality of their home circumstances or the care of the workhouse or prison, Carpenter, Barnado, and others tried increasingly to identify the ingredient missing in institutional care by comparing it with normal family life. The ingredient they came to identify was described as a failure to draw out and build on an individual's 'affections' – a process which was seen as a natural part of a good home life and vital to the development of sound character. It did not fit easily into the disciplined 'training' or 'educational' approaches of the large workhouse or new specialist child care establishments.

When Barnado opened a voluntary home for destitute boys in 1870, it was modelled on a 'barrack system'; a disciplined, work-centred routine designed to provide physical care and occupational training as well as inculcating good social habits. He used the same model three years later when he opened a home for girls, but this did not in practice achieve such good results and in considering the reasons for this Barnado had a vision:

> 'Instead of a big house, with sixty girls clad in dull uniform I would arrange for a number of little ivy clad cottages to arise, each presided over by a kindly, Christian woman who would be the "Mother". The children should be all ages, from the baby-in-arms to the girl well on in her teens training for service. They should be dressed as simply and with as much variety as possible and there should be nothing in the way of uniform. Anything approaching institutionalism would be scrupulously excluded. In such a home and in such an atmosphere, the affectionate ties of family life and family love would have a chance of being created and fostered in the experience of the children, while the daily performance of commonplace duties would tend to fit them for their future career. Surely the family is God's way for "He setteth the solitary in families".'
> (Wagner 1979 : 121)

It was a vision suggesting that, in emulating normal home life residential units could promote a girl's capacity for both affection and steady work. It was a vision that encouraged the establishment of 'cottage homes' – smaller residential units, headed by a housemother and grouped in villages – which were to become a characteristic part of child care provision over the next seventy years.

At a time, then, when most residential care was shaped by models that drew on custodial, militaristic, or punitive ideas, the 'family model' was seen as one that was appropriate only to the most 'deserving' elements. Thus, apart from children, it was elderly and disabled individuals selected by voluntary organizations as suitable to live outside the workhouse, who received the benefit of more 'homelike' residential environments.

When the notion of 'family' or 'home' life on which these establishments were attempting to model themselves is examined it is seen to be tied as closely to concerns about work discipline and self-reliance as the regimes it was attempting to replace. The rationale behind attempts to engage the 'affections' of children and young people through 'mothering' rested on a view that this would increase their commitment to the training and discipline it was necessary to offer in order to build character and establish the virtues of self-reliance. For other groups, dependent, but deserving, and no longer able to offer themselves for work, comforts unknown in the workhouse were provided on the clear understanding that they were a reward for a life of toil and thrift; and this message was often reinforced through the daily religious activities of many voluntary homes.

This model of family life, used as a positive inspiration in some residential regimes at the end of the nineteenth century and through to the Second World War, was a limited one. It was shaped by a desire to provide a residential environment which was successful in instilling the virtues of independence and work in those whose natural families had failed them. The key to this was seen to be in replicating the mother–child relationship in daily inmate–staff interaction. It developed in practice in a very limited fashion.

When the Curtis Committee reviewed the whole spectrum of residential care for children in 1946, its report showed clearly that in the area where concern to use a family model of care had been strongest, it had had very little impact on the daily residential experience of staff and residents. The Committee noted a lack of attention to individual needs; a lack of toys and leisure pursuits; an emphasis on domestic tasks for both staff and children; and little contact with the world outside the institution, not only in workhouses and barrack schools but also in cottage and scattered homes. Indeed, the residential establishments which drew most praise from the committee were those which had based their approach to caring on a very different model – the Approved Schools.

The Committee was pessimistic in its conclusions about the possibilities of developing a range of residential solutions modelled on family care. In its view it is only in 'the free conditions of ordinary family life with its opportunities for varied human contacts and experience, that the child's nature develops and his confidence in life and ease in society are established in a way which can hardly be achieved in a larger establishment being as it must a more strictly regulated existence.'

As a consequence, the Committee stressed the need for specialist children's departments which would try to use ordinary families to provide substitute homes rather than institutions. However, for those children for whom such homes could not be found residential communities should be developed which aimed to make 'as good a substitute for the private home as it can possibly be'. The path for achieving this lay in organizing the residential care of children on 'family group' lines. Mixed age and sex groups of no more than twelve children who would be cared for, if possible, by a married couple – the wife being in charge of the home, whilst the husband pursued a job outside. This plan, the committee concluded 'comes nearest to reproducing the actual conditions of family life', particularly if the group is living in an ordinary house in the community.

The committee's approach to reviewing and recommending changes in residential care for children drew on a model of family life which differed in a number of ways from that which had dominated pre-war thinking on residential child care practice. It criticized existing practice for not providing children with the opportunities of family life – ordinary, every-day experiences of leisure and domestic activity, and room for individual growth and social and emotional development. It represented a clear shift from stressing those elements of family life which 'trained character' and disciplined its members for their future occupational roles, to stressing those elements which nurtured the emotional and social needs of its individual members.

The alternative model of residential care the committee suggested reflected this shift. It attempted to set up in residential establishments a replica of the privatized world of the nuclear family. Relatively small groups of children, at various stages of development, cared for in ordinary housing by a couple whose occupations reflected a sexual division of labour. This was in the committee's view the way to provide as normal an upbringing as possible outside the family.

Where attempts were made to realize this new vision in practice, its limits became rapidly apparent. Staff prepared to carry out this task could not be assured of a settled group of children to live with. The emphasis the new children's departments placed on maintaining children in the community and on working to return children in care to their own families inevitably increased requests to residential establishments for short-term care and 'holding' operations. The changes in legislation in the 1960s which resulted in an integration of resources for children in trouble with the courts and those in need of substitute homes, increased the range of 'individual needs' residential establishments were expected to meet. In this new climate, family group homes became a residential solution which was seen as appropriate only to a narrow range of children. The stresses on staff in cramped accommodation and isolated working situations which seemed to demand a seven-day-a-week commitment, took their toll in turnover figures. Despite these problems, the popularity of the family model of residential care continued to spread beyond the child care field. As it was stressed that 'family was best' for a wide range of dependent groups, attention was turned to developing more 'home-like' and 'family' atmospheres in residential provision for offenders, the mentally disordered, the physically handicapped, and the elderly.

For the Williams Committee, reporting on the state of residential care in the 1960s, one of the major reasons for this shift was the gradual replacement of large-scale by small-scale institutions. These, intended to provide more individualized care and experience of ordinary daily living, were based naturally, at first, on an image of an extended family group run by a mother (or occasionally a father).

Added to this, was the emphasis during this period on the key importance of the emotional elements of family life. Residential communities based on family group lines were seen as providing therapeutic opportunities for individuals to mature emotionally and to come to terms with their life situations. In due course, offenders, unmarried mothers, the elderly, and others besides children, were seen as being able to make use of such a residential experience, which by providing a stable base and skilled help could compensate for the lack of emotional support from their own family situations.

One of the problems, however, of the stress on family models of residential care lay in the idea it conveyed of the task of the residential worker. When the Williams Committee reported in 1967 it stated its alarm at the frequency with which it had encountered the 'misconception that residential care is just the same as the work of every family but on a larger scale'. It pointed out that this resulted in the work of residential staff being seen as 'more or less the same sort of job as that done by any housewife with a fairly large family (Williams 1967 : 30). With its concern to develop professional identity and professional training in the residential field, the Williams Committee attempted to establish that crucial differences did exist between the skills required by residential workers and those employed by 'ordinary' families. Since 1967 these differences have been elaborated, as a growing professional literature has sought to establish the similarity between residential work and social work. Yet problems continue to emerge in holding a balance between the 'professional' and 'parenting' elements of the residential task; problems which residential workers are left to resolve in their daily encounters with residents.

The relationship, then, between residential care and the family, has been and continues to be a complex one. Notions of what family life provides for the individual have been constantly used to criticize the practice and outcome of a great deal of residential care. Throughout the nineteenth and twentieth centuries the 'tension' which Goffman identifies between the care environment of the family and the institution has been very apparent in comparisons that have been made between the private and individualized world of the former and the public and regimented world of the latter (Goffman 1961). In the post-war period attention has increasingly focused on loss of personal identity entailed in moving from the first world to the second – through the 'tunnel of betrayal' as Goffman calls it. This comparison between family care and residential care has led some to query whether residential provision can ever be of any positive value to the individual. Those who believe it cannot, have argued that resources going into residential care should be redirected towards strengthening family and community care. Yet, at the same time, others have seen a way forward through residential care being brought closer in scale and style to family care – and this has been attempted by some workers in practice.

What has emerged from their experiences is an awareness of the difficulties of trying to replicate family-style relationships in situations where paid staff and residents live together for a wide variety of reasons. As a result the more 'personalized' relationships of these units have not always been found to be as enriching as the notion, on which they were based, suggested. The family model of residential practice appears to be a limited one, because the assumptions on which it has developed have not paid as much attention to the *content* of family living as they have to its *form*. The suggestion has been that if the form is right – a small unit; an ordinary daily routine; 'mother' (and perhaps 'father') figures; homely surroundings – then the content will follow, through the opportunities provided for more individualized relationships. Both workers and residents have discovered it as not as easy as that.

Summary

This chaper has examined some of the implications for residential workers of providing a welfare service which has the potential to remove care responsibilities from the sphere of individual family life. The argument has been that residential workers are operating in a policy and practice context shaped by a number of implicit and contradictory assumptions about the relationship between family and residential care.

At a policy level, some of these assumptions have led to a view that good quality residential care might undermine the willingness of families to care for their dependent members, whilst others have led to an emphasis on the function residential care performs in protecting individuals and the social order from the contaminating influence of certain families. The balance of these assumptions has been such that a tradition has emerged that residential care is a residual resource, to be used as a last resort, on a declaration of individual and family failure.

At a practice level, notions of family life have proved to be an important reference point for developing residential regimes. Criticisms of residential care have tended to be based on negative contrasts between family and institutional life. At the same time, attempts have been made by some practitioners to close the gap by developing residential units which model their structure and routine on family life.

The implication of these considerations is that residential workers need to consider their theory and practice in the context of the welfare system of which they are a part; for this system reflects ideas and sustains policies which make conflicting and contradictory demands upon residential units, demands which residential workers are left to negotiate daily.

3

Family-substitute care

Classification of residential provision

Having looked at some of the general issues the state provision of residential care raises, this and the next two chapters consider the current range of residential provision in Britain. It is difficult, when one looks across this range, to find a useful way of classifying the residential units it includes, although it is relatively easy to find reasons for rejecting existing classifications. Grouping units in terms of the client group they serve tends to neglect the experiences, tasks, and aims which residential workers have in common; grouping them in terms of the purposes they are formally declared to be serving (for example, observation and assessment, rehabilitation, or long-term care) ignores the fact that, in practice, very different purposes tend to evolve. Staff definitions of purpose do not seem any more useful; as the Personal Social Services Council (PSSC) study of residential provision for adults demonstrated, many residential staff appear to have little idea of the overall purpose of the units in which they work and live (PSSC 1975).

The classification I have chosen to adopt is one that reflects my concern with the relationship between family and residential care. It therefore groups existing provision in terms of the function it serves in relation to the family. I have three main reasons for suggesting this approach.

First, as I have indicated, views about the basis on which the relationship between residential care and family care should rest have been of fundamental importance to the development of state residential provision in this country (Kammerman and Kahan 1978 : 331).

Second, social workers have come to be seen increasingly as family workers. A major task thrust upon local authority social services departments (the main providers of state residential care) has been one of providing a family service. In recent years, too, the probation service has expressed an increasing interest in the influence of family environment on the behaviour of individual offenders. Ideas of assessing, supporting, and strengthening the family are central to current social work thinking. If residential care is ever to become part of the strategy of social work, then a consideration of residential work in the light of this emphasis on family support is crucial.

Third, recent discussions in Britain about welfare provision in general, and residential care in particular, have reflected concern about the consequences of current changes in population and family structures. Increased life expectancy, changing marriage patterns, mobility, and the changing role of women, have all raised questions about the caring capacity of the family and the demands likely to be made on it, as welfare expenditure is limited. It is, therefore, important to assess the current role of residential care in relation to the family, in order to gain some perspective on the likely consequences of future developments.

A first step in this direction is to identify the stance residential units take in relation to the 'natural' support and control networks of the family. (The term 'family' is here used to refer in a 'shorthand' way to the household unit which takes responsibility for the management of its individual members.)

I suggest that three major positions can be taken. First, a unit can be seen as offering a *substitute* for family care; the provision of care and control for individuals, replacing family support. Second, a unit can be seen as offering a *supplement* to family care; the use of a residential environment as a means of strengthening the family's efforts to manage its members. Third, a unit can be seen as offering an *alternative* to family care; the provision of a residential environment designed to establish a communal way of life as an alternative to, rather than a substitute for, family life.

In distinguishing between these stances I am not ruling out the possibility that some units might attempt to pursue two, if not all three, simultaneously. Neither am I suggesting that all units and their staff have explicitly adopted, and are working towards, a particular stance. The value, as I see it, of making this kind of distinction is that it provides some useful insights into the implications for both staff and residents of working and living in units which inevitably adopt particular stances towards the family.

Family-substitute care is examined in this chapter; family-alternative care in chapter four, and family-supplement care in chapter five. Each chapter outlines the underlying assumptions, reviews the type of provision offered, and suggests what problems and potential each raises for residential workers.

The definition of family-substitute care and its problems

Residential units striving to provide care which is at least as good as the family care individual residents have previously experienced, are offering family-substitute care. They vary in size, care philosophies, and practice. Their staff express diverse views about the nature of dependency, deviance, and institutional and family life. Their residents come from all age groups. Yet what they hold in common, as residential solutions, is an aspiration to model their regimes, and through them, their care practices, on 'ordinary family life'. They are attempting to meet the needs of residents in the way in which a family might meet those needs, by trying to reflect in their daily routines the rhythms of family life and by trying to provide the kind of emotional experiences which are a normal part of family membership.

In attempting to provide a substitute for family care the staff of such units find themselves faced with a number of common problems. While some of these are general to units of any kind, some arise specifically from the task family-substitute units are attempting to fulfil. Four of these have been selected for consideration. They are: (1) the impact of entry to this kind of care; (2) the relationship between residents, workers, and family; (3) the appropriateness of this kind of care for all client groups; and (4) the links between family-substitute units and the wider community.

Entry into family-substitute care

Usually, residential workers in this type of unit are expected to care for individuals who have been judged to be 'in need' of family-substitute care by others, often their fieldwork colleagues. Residential workers play little part in this selection process although experience and research has shown that the admission of particular individuals can have a dramatic impact on the group dynamics of a residential unit.

Of course, once admission takes place, residential workers can attempt to control the repercussions of an individual's influence on the group in various ways and can, in the last resort, exclude him or her.

The strategies used to handle the impact of admission on the new resident, staff, and established residents, vary. Some units tackle the question as one of ensuring that the unit's regime is maintained. The opportunity for new residents to express their feelings about admission are restricted and emphasis is placed on learning the rules, routines, and expectations which the unit has of new members. Other units stress that the potential benefit to individual residents from their stay is dependent on the way in which they are worked with on admission. Focusing on such feelings as anger, depression, and shame, and accepting and responding to behaviour such as regression, is seen as part of the task which workers take on with each new admission. Entry to care, it has been argued, can be usefully conceived as a personal crisis, which given the right kind of support can be a personally enhancing experience. An individual's adaptation to the life of the unit and the resident group is therefore seen as stemming from this type of staff response to admission.

In a number of ways this stance marks a positive step in residential work. Long-established traditions associated with entry into residential units, concerned with the batch 'processing' of residents to fit the existing regime, are challenged. The validity of a number of care practices which strip individuals of their previous identities in order to enhance the efficient functioning of the unit are questioned. Staff become sensitized to the impact of entry on each resident and the need to consider that impact as part of each individual's life experience. The implications that a well-handled entry to care has for the future use of residential communities by their members are highlighted.

At the same time, however, this stance has its drawbacks. It can focus residential workers' attention so intensely on the problems of individual adjustment to the unit, that the social nature of the selection process which residents have been through is forgotten. It can reinforce the idea that residential workers should take on trust that individuals who have been selected to enter their care are suffering from the kind of individual or family pathology which justifies the use of this welfare resource.

In fact, as a number of recent studies have shown, individuals continue to be selected for entry to family-substitute residential care because of a lack in their own families and communities of such basic resources as adequate housing, income, health, and education services (Holman 1980; Taylor, Lacey, and Bracken 1979). For such individuals the offer of residential care of a family-substitute kind may not be the most appropriate response to need. Indeed, removing them from their own homes and working with them at adjusting to family-substitute care may close a number of options which could be used in their long-term interests. Feelings of anger, shame, despair, or depression in an individual resident may reflect as much a rational response to this predicament as it reflects the immediate impact of the units' regime and separation from family or community life.

As staff in family-substitute residential units are not usually involved in exploring alternative care and support options for potential residents or their families, they may find themselves attempting to fulfil a task prescribed by others which, despite their own efforts, is not the most appropriate response to a client's problems. In such a situation their own practice skills may be strait-jacketed at an early stage by decisions made by other workers and agencies.

For example, there is now considerable evidence to suggest that many families who experience difficulties in caring for dependent members, are looking for support – a means of sharing care, or short-term relief – not a total relief from carrying caring responsibilities. Yet R. Moroney, who looked at families providing care for the elderly and mentally handicapped (Moroney 1976), shows how requests from families for anything less than long-term institutional care tend to be ignored by the welfare services. Similarly, Bayley's study of the family care of mentally handicapped adults found that field social workers rarely gear available welfare services to supplementing and supporting families who are providing social care (Bayley 1973).

Such findings reflect a pattern in Britain in which state services tend 'either to assume major or complete responsibility for the care of the dependant, or to leave that responsibility squarely and unambiguously with the family' (Kammerman and Kahan 1978 : 331). As a vital part of that pattern, residential units are being continuously drawn on to make provision which may not, in fact, meet the needs being expressed by the resident or his or her family. It is likely that residential workers may be faced with the personal repercussion of this each time they welcome a new resident to their unit.

The family and the unit

Issues which arise from the use of family-substitute care are not just confined to the way in which the individual and the residential unit relate. For in most family-substitute units, particularly those for children and young people, there are a number of residents who still have families of their own. Some of these families may have been relieved of their care responsibilities because they have been judged to be unfit for the task. Others may well have declared themselves unable or unwilling to carry on caring for particular members. Yet others may have experienced social or personal difficulties for which the residential care of a particular individual was the only solution available.

As substitutes, in the short or long term for these families, residential workers will inevitably be faced with the question of how they should relate to them. What part should they be playing in the ongoing relationship between residents and their families?

It is in the residential child care literature that this question has received the fullest consideration.

The ideas promoted by the Curtis Report in its review of residential care for children in 1946, are a starting point from which to trace current working assumptions. In pointing to a new direction for the state provision of residential child care in the post-war era, this report suggested that residential workers should attempt to become substitute parents for those children entering public care and that the units in which they worked should be organized on the lines of 'ordinary family homes'. However, as the viability of this notion was costed and tested in a limited way in residential practice, it was increasingly questioned. The continuous demands made on care staff, the lack of a settled group of children, cramped accommodation, and the problems of meeting individual need in a small group, were all identified as drawbacks to implementing Curtis-style family group homes on a wide scale. At the same time, changes in the aims of the child care services appeared to place fresh demands on residential units. In particular, the emphasis on working to maintain children with their natural families led increasingly to the view that the main task of residential units should be for 'short-term' or 'holding' care, with a view to rehabilitating and resettling children in the community with their own or a foster family (Packman 1975). As residential child care units have come to be seen as 'interim' rather than 'long-term' substitutes for family care, residential staff have been asked *not* to attempt to become substitutes for the child's natural parents. Yet, at the same time, they have also been asked to ensure that they undertake 'parenting' in all its aspects, in order to provide a residential environment that is responsive to each child's social and emotional needs. As Christopher Beedell has put it:

> 'We must use parental and familial words . . . or we shall deny some of the emotional and social realities of residential work. On the other hand we must use them with greater intellectual and emotional discrimination.'   (Beedell 1970 : 135)

In practice, of course, it cannot be guaranteed that all children placed in residential care return to families before reaching adulthood, and so the function of most family-substitute units is more 'mixed' than 'interim'. As a consequence, residential workers are expected to 'parent without becoming parents' for extended periods of some children's lifetimes. J. Berry sums up the situation as one in which workers are 'exhorted to be parental and non-parental, simultaneously' (Berry 1975 : 13) – a difficult if not impossible, balance to establish and retain. It does little to clarify the views staff hold of the task they are undertaking and of the relationship such a task bears to a child's own family. Residential workers are being asked to develop relationships and caring environments which have the emotional depth of family situations, but which do not act as a barrier between the resident and his natural family.

It is hardly surprising that many residential workers, engaged in prolonged and at times, intense, contact with clients in units implicitly designed to do what their families could or would not do, tend to lose sight of this goal. Although there is little research in this area, experience suggests that many staff engaged in family-substitute care develop negative attitudes towards residents' families. In a sense, these reflect nothing more than a share in the predominant attitudes held in Britain towards those who relinquish the care of those for whom they are responsible. However, when one is working and living with residents, such attitudes can be reinforced by more personal feelings, such as attachment to an individual resident and subsequent rivalry with the natural family.

Intense feelings are not the sole prerogative of residential workers. Docker-Drysdale, in her discussion of the parents of maladjusted children in residential care, suggests that it is the parents' feelings of inadequacy in having to allow outsiders to care for their children which can result in displays of hostility and envy towards a unit and its staff (Docker-Drysdale 1973 : 23). McCormack, in her review of residential provision for the mentally handicapped, also suggests that criticism from families often derives from their concern at the poor quality of care provided for their relatives (McCormack 1979).

Staff, faced with such responses from residents' families about their care of residents, are quite likely to deal with them by reminding themselves (and sometimes residents and their families) that 'at least' they are still caring when the family has failed. This is hardly an attitude which is likely to enhance resident and family contact.

Staff, too, are liable to be in frequent contact with the feelings of residents towards their own families. If these are strongly negative, then staff will more naturally accept them than confront them. If these are strongly positive, then staff may interpret them either as a criticism of the substitute care which they are offering, or as a failure on the part of the resident to face 'reality' and adapt to his or her current situation.

These attitudes need to be explicitly discussed and challenged if residential workers are to play any part in strengthening or maintaining the links between residents and their families.

White's account of Mill Grove, a voluntary residential home for children which offers family-substitute care (Payne and White 1979 : 74), describes one approach to tackling this problem. Admission to the unit is limited to 'children whose home situation has been admitted by all concerned, including the parents, to have broken down irretrievably for the foreseeable future' (Payne and White 1979 : 83). With this established, contact with parents is encouraged on the basis that the unit is the new home base and that the parents' new role is to support that base. Staff acknowledge that this is 'a hard and sometimes traumatic task', but argue that it is a necessary one if a child is to learn that his or her substitute home is going to prove to be secure and stable.

Obviously this approach is not one which would be acceptable to every family-substitute unit, but it does suggest that something is to be gained from clarifying and, if possible, agreeing to the kind of contact which it is appropriate to establish between residents, workers, and families.

The appropriateness of family-substitute care

When family-substitute care is offered in the absence of a family the mandate to residential workers is less ambiguous. They are expected to fill a gap as completely as they are able and, in doing so, they need to assess how appropriate their care is for the residents for whom they are responsible.

There are two strands in the recent debates about family-substitute units for those without family which are relevant to consider here. First, some of the literature appears to stress the value of using residential units to reproduce the close relationships akin to family life in order to provide a therapeutic experience for individuals whose own problems centre on a failure to initiate or sustain family ties. Sinclair (1971) refers to this in relation to the debate on hostel provision for young offenders and it has also been part of approaches to such groups as the mentally disordered. Second, the concern which has emerged in social work over the last two decades for ensuring that, within residential units for adults, the worth and dignity of the individual resident is recognized has often been expressed through analogy with the 'good' or 'normal' family. In this way, the recognition of the common social and emotional needs of residents has been seen as emerging through the provision of more 'homely' or 'family-like' environments in which opportunities are provided for workers to relate to small groups of residents.

What is often far from clear is how this assumption, that the most appropriate model for the care of adults is one of family life, is to be worked through in practice. In a number of ways, a stress on the worth of dignity of each individual resident and the provision of opportunities which will maximize his or her potential to reach as 'normal' an adult status as possible, seems to jostle uneasily with a vision of residential communities which attempt to simulate familial relationships.

There is evidence that certain groups of dependent adults are inhibited in exploring their potential for independence by the attitudes and behaviour of their own families, yet the implications of this have received limited consideration by residential workers who see the use of the family analogy as a positive development in this area of residential care. Indeed, at times, the descriptions of the type of relationships which workers should aspire to establish with residents draw so heavily on a 'parent-child' model that they come close to infantilizing adult residents.

Work remains to be done to establish just how productive it is to seek to re-create family structures in residential units. After all, as many social workers have found, the relationships and power structures inherent in family life are not always enabling; they also generate and sustain emotional difficulties in individual members.

At the same time, workers should reflect on the fact that in offering care of a family-substitute kind they are expected to work in 'family groups' which are often open-ended. Such groups are added to (if not subtracted from) as the result of decisions in which those directly responsible for providing care may have only a marginal say. As the dynamics of such a group will change with each new addition and departure (particularly if the substitute care offered is short-term), workers are constantly called on to respond to changes in individual and group needs.

In these situations a sense of coherence and stability may be impossible to retain. The use of family analogies by workers to understand and direct their efforts may be self-defeating. It could be that, for some workers, discarding the family analogy may enable them to look at their work for what it is: the care and control of dependent, disabled, and deviate individuals in a public care situation of which there are conflicting expectations.

The unit and the community

Finally, workers in family-substitute units are faced with the fact that the experience of 'family life' is not one which is confined just to close relatives and their household. It also encompasses territories, and networks of friends and pursuits, which are based in the community and these are at times as significant for individual well-being as the family unit. Entry to any form of residential care often involves a severing of these links with no guarantee to the individual that they will be replaced in the 'care' situation. But if workers are concerned to provide as good a substitute for family care as possible they need to take into account this aspect of individual and group life.

Increasing reference in recent years has been made in the policy and professional literature to the importance of establishing links with the surrounding community so that it can be used as a resource for family-substitute units. There have been very few accounts of the extent to which this has been pursued and achieved in practice.

The location of the unit can have a significant influence here. A building which is separate from its local community, by distance or extensive grounds, may be more difficult to 'open up' than a building which is part of a local street. Yet it does not necessarily follow that staff and residents in the latter will automatically establish the kind of links with the local community that will enable residents to replace the friendship networks they may have lost, or build them for the first time. Residents may be too handicapped or physically frail to move outside their unit without risk and, as Brown has pointed out in his discussion of elderly persons' homes, concern about the public ac-countability of residential units can result in staff avoiding risk-taking of this kind (Brown 1974 : 135).

There are other kinds of risks involved here too. In some com-munities, residential units which are 'open' can attract friends and visitors whose demands may, at times, upset the unit's attempts to cater for its own residents' needs and whose behaviour may alienate members of the local community. In the long term, units can also generate a local network of former residents by becoming a focus for groups who find they have nowhere else to go socially. This can have repercussions on the kind of contacts the unit and its current residents are able to make with neighbours and the local community.

Again, there are relatively few guidelines for workers to follow in developing an approach in their own units to this issue. On the one hand, it is clear that residential units cannot provide all that an individual resident requires to enjoy life and fulfil his, or her, poten-tial. On the other hand, opening up links with the local community, using 'outside' resources, and encouraging the participation of 'out-siders' in the life of the unit, can at times increase the situations of risk and uncertainty to which residential workers have to respond. As *state* substitutes for family care, residential units and their staff are open to public comment and scrutiny on this issue in a way which most families are not. In working through ways of living in close contact with local communities, workers need to anticipate the influence this will have on their plans.

The potential of family-substitute care

Having considered a few of the key problems workers face in attempting to use residential provision to simulate family care, the remainder of this chapter considers the potential of this sort of care. As I said in chapter one, judgements on this are dependent on the view taken about the effect of social work approaches on the practice of workers and about the role of residential provision in the welfare system. It is with this debate in mind, that the discussion about potential in this chapter and the next two takes place.

There is a very real sense in which it seems absurd to attempt to provide family-substitute care in residential units, when it might be possible to extend the use of substitute families in the community to a number of client groups. Rowe and Lambert's study *Children Who Wait* indicated that thousands of children currently in residential care could move out if fostering were more actively developed (Rowe and Lambert 1973). Several studies of the residents of elderly persons' homes have suggested that the expansion of sheltered housing would result in a decrease in the numbers in residential care (Townsend 1977). Recent contributions to discussions about the mentally and physically disabled suggest that fostering, boarding-out schemes, and adapted housing, could all play a part in reducing the demand for residential care (Kings Fund 1980).

However, although the indications are that a great deal more can be done in this area, it is unlikely that residential care of a family-substitute kind is likely to become redundant. For particular individuals in particular circumstances it will continue to be seen as the best solution to those circumstances. It is therefore important for workers involved in this kind of care to begin to identify the conditions in which family-substitute care is an appropriate response to individual and family difficulty. They must also identify the best conditions for providing daily experiences, for residents and themselves, that reflect a way of life at least as good as that which ordinary families enjoy.

Several recent studies have indicated that in residential units, as in other complex organizations, there appears to be no logical connection between formal task, unit regime, and worker practices. Until residential workers can tackle these connections, the potential of family-substitute care is likely to remain only partially realized.

It seems that it is only by systematic observation of the pattern of daily client-worker interaction that a judgement can be made about what is meant by substituting for family care in any one unit. It is for this reason that residential workers who are involved in offering family-substitute care, need to be able to stand aside and look at their daily encounters in order to develop and extend their practice.

There are tools available to do this which have been developed in the course of two studies of substitute-family care, the first concerned with the care of handicapped children (King, Raynes, and Tizard 1971), the second with handicapped adults (Raynes, Pratt, and Roses 1979). Both have viewed the variation in care practices which have evolved in this area of residential provision as ranging from 'institution-oriented' practice to 'resident-oriented' practice. The former is defined as practice aimed at ensuring an efficient, smoothly-running unit; the latter as practice aimed at creating a residential environment responsive to individual needs of both residents and staff. These represent polar positions on a spectrum and most units providing family-substitute care will fall between the two. The usefulness of this approach to residential work is that it is concerned to identify certain key features of a unit's daily routine, in order to establish the practice orientation. It is observations such as these which provide the kind of data staff could use to test out practice ideas. This kind of approach could also sharpen attempts to change practice within particular units, in order to establish family-substitute regimes.

The features which both studies identify and develop as crucial to establishing the orientation of a unit are: rigidity of routine; block treatment; depersonalization; and social distance.

Rigidity of routine refers to the degree to which the daily regime of a unit responds to differences in circumstances and residents. When regimes do not take account of changes in circumstances and the individual responses of residents, they reflect an institution-oriented approach; when a response is made to these factors then it reflects a resident-oriented approach. The organization of meal times, sleeping times, variety and changes in leisure activities, can all be used as indicators of where a unit falls on the spectrum.

Block treatment of residents describes the way in which the unit deals with residents. If, for example, residents are treated as a group for such activities as feeding, toileting, and bathing – then practice is institutionally-oriented. Conversely, where residents have a choice in the extent to which they participate in such activities and have time to tackle them at their own pace, then practice is resident-oriented.

Depersonalization refers to the degree to which opportunities exist for residents to have personal privacy, personal possessions, and a chance to initiate activities which are personally important. Institutionally-oriented units will limit these areas, whilst resident-oriented units will maximize opportunities for individuals to express themselves in these ways.

Similarly with social distance, units which encourage demarcation between the worlds of staff and residents – with regard to both physical and emotional needs – reflect institutionally-oriented practice. Units in which such things as space, facilities, and leisure time are shared between staff and residents reflect a resident-orientation.

If this approach is considered alongside current social work thinking, then the values underlying a 'resident-oriented' regime appear synonymous with the values and objectives expressed by the social work profession. It follows that, if social workers are to use family-substitute residential care as part of their response to families and individuals in difficulty, then the kind of care offered should aspire to provide environments which minimize rigidity of routine, block treatment, depersonalization, and social distance.

STAFF AND STRESS

The problems faced by workers in realizing and sustaining these kinds of environment can be considerable. Menzies, Miller and Gwynne, and others have suggested that institution-oriented regimes provide defences for staff against stress (Menzies 1960; Miller and Gwynne 1972). It follows that the personal and individualized contact with residents generated by resident-oriented practice may result in staff and residents in units experiencing increased tension and conflict. Sinclair's study in the mid-sixties of hostels for young male probationers offers some important insights into the difficulties likely to be encountered (Sinclair 1971).

Sinclair found that in the hostels he looked at very close analogies could be drawn between the influence wardens and their wives had on resident behaviour and that which parents have on the behaviour of their delinquent sons. Such influence was the result, he argues, of the intense relationships formed between these chief care-givers and their charges; relationships generating the kind of 'ups and downs' in daily living which are an inevitable feature of family life. However, the staff primarily involved in providing these family-substitute experiences – the warden and his wife – were faced with conflicts and difficulties qualitatively different from those faced by parents. These problems, Sinclair suggests, arose from the fact that care was being provided for a large group of young men in a situation which was publicly account-able. As a result, staff found themselves working in demanding and socially isolated conditions and this put considerable strain on their health, marriages, and families. From his observations Sinclair con-cludes that the provision of family-substitute care raises 'peculiar problems' for staff. It is an approach to caring which combines stresses arising from intimate, family-like relationships with stresses arising from managing an institution in which workers cannot resort to the usual kind of institutional defences.

Apart from grappling with the interpersonal demands made by this kind of care, residential workers need, also, to be aware of the organizational and policy constraints they face in developing the potential of resident-oriented care. Research findings suggest that these constraints are likely to include: the attitudes and training of the head of the unit; the organization and autonomy of the unit; the size and nature of the resident group.

ATTITUDES OF HEADS OF UNITS

To take the influence of the head of the unit as an example, the study by King and others of residential units catering for handicapped children suggests that the 'style' of practice adopted by unit heads has a clear influence on the care practices of other staff. The 'style' adopted by these unit heads reflected to a great degree their profes-sional training. Nurse-trained heads had less direct contact with residents and emphasized administrative and physical aspects of care; the orientation of their care staff reflected this. Child-care trained heads, on the other hand, emphasized the social and emotional needs of the children, and engaged in more direct contact with them; their care staff engaged in a wider range of activities with their residents (King, Raynes, and Tizard 1971). In contrast, the findings of other studies, such as Sinclair's study of probation hostels (Sinclair 1971) and Berry's study of residential units for children (Berry 1975) demonstrate a lack of correlation between the 'style' of the head of the unit and his or her training background.

Sinclair suggests that in the units he studied, it was possible to distinguish a style which was more successful in reducing the incidence of offending than others. This style did not reflect a particular kind of training, rather it reflected a combination in the unit head of certain personal and marital characteristics. Hostels which were successful in positively changing the behaviour of residents were found to be ones in which: 'The warden was very strict, clearly the dominant person in a hostel where his wife agreed with his policy and was characterized by a certain warmth towards his charges' (Tizard, Sinclair, and Clarke 1975 : 130).

AUTONOMY AND GROUP SIZE OF UNITS

Again, the issues of autonomy and group size in family-substitute units have proved to be more complex than many practitioners envisaged. One of the most popular suggestions for achieving an individualized approach in family-substitute care has been to break large residential units into smaller 'family groups', for which a member of staff has prime responsibility. The assumption has been that such a structure will provide staff and residents with a warmer, more supportive, group living experience. Yet research and practice experience has raised two questions about the potential of this approach.

First, small group living experiences have not proved flexible in coping with some individual behaviours. Sinclair suggests that one drawback of small family-substitute units is that:

'by devolving so much responsibility on one or two key members of staff, they make it less easy to ensure a uniform standard of performance and provide the residents with a smaller choice of adults to whom to relate. There may, therefore, be a greater risk that certain residents feel that the key members of staff have their knife

into them and they, themselves, have no respite and, indeed, the key members of staff may feel the equivalent.'
(Tizard, Sinclair, and Clarke 1975 : 129)

Second, as Raynes' study of residential units for mentally handicapped adults showed, small group living is no guarantee of an increase in resident-oriented care practice. In examining the range of practices used in the care of small groups of mentally handicapped adults, Raynes and her colleagues discovered that in some units institution-oriented practices continued to dominate daily living experiences. In explaining this continuance, Raynes suggests that factors such as the involvement of staff in decision-making, the authority invested in care staff, and the wider management and promotional systems of which the unit is a part, have a decisive influence. In her view: 'without a supportive organizational structure for care, staff innovations to improve the quality of care will neither endure nor contribute much to raise the standard of care' (Raynes, Pratt, and Roses 1979 : 60).

IMPLICATIONS FOR THE FUTURE

This suggests that developing the potential of family-substitute care is dependent on developing and sustaining care practices in tune with a resident-oriented approach to residential care. King and Raynes and their colleagues have developed a tool for identifying specific areas of practice where this can be done, but work with this will only achieve limited results if conducted in a vacuum. To realize the kind of residential environments which can offer a substitute for family care, residential staff need to sensitize themselves not only to the consequences of their daily practice for residents, but also to the connections between their daily practice and the wider organization of which they are part. As Raynes and Sinclair both point out, staff in family-substitute units can only deal creatively with the tensions and conflicts arising from a more individualized caring approach, if they have the right kind of organizational support.

Summary

This chapter has examined a number of issues raised by family-substitute care. The suggestion is that although the assumption underlying family-substitute care is that a family model can offer positive experiences to residents, there are considerable difficulties in realizing them in practice. These difficulties emerge in some of the problems workers encounter in responding to individuals who enter this kind of care. It is not often the case that family-substitute care is seen initially by residents to be a positive response to their problems. Yet residential workers are expected to offer care on the assumption that it is the best option in certain circumstances. In attempting to replicate family life in their units, workers are likely to be faced with problems of relating to the existing natural family networks of their residents. It is not easy to communicate with these networks when units are aiming to substitute for them. In the absence of guidelines, it becomes easy for staff to slip into relationships of rivalry or hostility with families, which inevitably influence the nature of the contact they are able to maintain with residents. In the absence of friends or family, the operation of this care approach becomes easier for workers to justify. However, the circumstances in which it is the most positive response to client need are still far from clear. The negative as well as the positive aspects of family life need to be considered by residential workers who are involved in developing their practice on family-substitute lines. Finally, any attempt to substitute for family life needs to take into account the community links which families sustain. Ensuring that residents are offered the opportunity to maintain such links can raise questions of risk and public accountability for workers which are qualitatively different from those faced by ordinary families.

In discussing the potential of this kind of care, it is important to recognize that it rests on the development of regimes which are responsive to the wishes of both residents and workers. It has been suggested that there are tools available which can help staff to change their practices in this direction, yet the use of these will not be sufficient in itself. The realization of family-type regimes is also heavily dependent on staff being given the kind of authority and organizational support which will allow them to take the kind of decisions and bear the brunt of the tensions of a 'normal' family life.

4

Family-alternative care

There is considerable variety in the forms of residential care which aim to provide a communal life, but not to replicate the family. Hospitals, schools, and prisons have each had a significant influence on family-alternative units. So have ideas derived from milieu therapy and the philosophies of alternative communities. Mixtures of these influences and ideas can be found in the regimes of units in which residential workers provide family-alternative care.

In the post-war period in Britain the varieties of this form of care have grown enormously. While it is impossible to draw up a definitive list of the models currently influencing family-alternative units, it may be possible to identify some of the more typical patterns which have evolved around particular client groups. Younghusband, for example, suggests that, apart from the family, the most positive analogy on which residential units for children have been based during this period has been the public school (Younghusband 1978 : 173). In contrast, the results of several studies of the regimes operating in elderly persons' homes, have demonstrated the influence of the model of hospital nursing on this form of care (Meacher 1972).

Because of the sheer diversity of the models on which family-alternative units draw, it is difficult to identify a set of practice assumptions which *all* share. However, what is clear is that all hold common assumptions about the family which distinguish them from family-substitute units, on the one hand, and family-supplement care on the other.

Core assumptions of family-alternative care

The core assumptions underlying the provision of family-alternative care, stress the limitations of family care and the pathological nature of some forms of family life. These assumptions tend to locate problems of individual functioning and behaviour in conditions generated in family life. In doing so they point to the need in certain circumstances for residential care which provides safety, protection, and an alternative way of life for particular individuals.

Such beliefs have a long tradition in the history of residential care. As I pointed out in chapter two, there was in the nineteenth century a strand in the debate about family responsibility and residential care which continuously contrasted the contaminating influence of particular forms of family and community life with the wholesome environment of particular forms of residential care. This tradition has been most marked in discussions about residential solutions to criminal behaviour and deprived children, but it has also permeated debates about other groups. Currently these ideas are in uneasy conflict with the stress put on the positive features of the family by the exponents of community care. Recent studies by Millham and Taylor and their colleagues suggest that this tradition is still a dominant theme in areas of our residential services (Millham, Bullock and Cherrett 1975; Millham, Bullock, and Hosie 1978; Taylor, Lacey, and Bracken 1980).

Alongside the view that family care and social life can contaminate individuals and engender deviant behaviours, there has also been an emphasis on the possibility of the reverse process occurring. Wilkins, in his discussion of the professional perspectives on mental handicap and family life, points to a tradition which has suggested that mental handicap in an individual family member can result in family pathology. The process is a simple one. The family is unable to respond 'normally' to what is an 'abnormal' condition in one of its members; its inadequate and limited responses result in a skew and stress in family relationships. In other words, the conditions of individual handicap have damaging effects on family life (Wilkins 1979 : 30). Those, such as Kew, who promote this view argue that the provision of specialist residential alternatives to the family is the best response to the handicapped individual, as well as a method of protecting the family itself from breakdown (Kew 1975).

The core assumptions of family alternative care are ones which emphasize the negative rather than the positive aspects of family life. They contrast markedly with the assumptions on which family-substitute and family-supplement care are based, for it is suggested that alternative communal living arrangements, organized on non-familial lines, can be a positive and preferred response to a range of individual difficulties.

In looking at the ways in which units have built on these core assumptions, it is possible to identify two distinct approaches. Some units have modelled their regimes on traditional, non-familial, residential institutions, while others have sought to develop regimes which provide an alternative to both the family *and* traditional institutional arrangements. This has resulted in a contrasting set of organizational and practice assumptions.

TRADITIONAL ASSUMPTIONS

Where family-alternative units have modelled their regimes on those of traditional and established institutions, they have justified their choice on the basis that these embody the type of institutional arrangements best able to meet the special needs of particular kinds of resident. The choices made reflect the selection and promotion of particular assumptions about the nature and causation of individual social problems. They may also reflect a preference for a particular professional or administrative response to those problems. For example, where the difficulties experienced by individuals in old age are seen primarily in terms of physical functioning, units are likely to pursue an approach to caring which, in focusing on physical care, takes on the organizational features of hospitals. Where the same difficulties are interpreted as a declining ability to provide the basics of domestic life, then units may well attempt to make provision modelled on a hotel or guest house regime. With residential provision for young people who have been involved in criminal activities some units may favour explanations of their behaviour which point to inadequate education and socialization and therefore adopt a boarding school approach to their residential care in order to make up for this deficiency. Other units may well see a lack of experience of discipline as being central to an understanding of this behaviour, and may therefore pursue a regime modelled on army life in seeking to redress the balance.

In adopting and developing such established patterns of care and control as a means of providing non-familial residential experiences, residential workers accept the staffing structures which are embodied in them. Such structures tend to reflect assumptions about the appropriate division of staff tasks as well as the appropriate sets of relationships which should be established between staff and residents. Because these are usually an implicit part of traditions, it is important that the implications they have for care practices are explicitly recognized by staff involved in them.

ALTERNATIVE ASSUMPTIONS

Some family-alternative units have developed an approach to caring which not only adopts a critical stance to family life but also questions the form of traditional patterns of institutional care. Such units are comparatively few in number, but their importance lies in their pioneering work in developing residential experiences which attempt to break new ground in communal living arrangements. The assumptions on which these units have drawn include the ideas promoted in the growth of therapeutic communities, as well as those promoted in communities which have sought to explore alternative life styles.

The content and origins of the ideas which have shaped the development of therapeutic communities in Britain have been well documented by M. Jones, J. Morrice, N. Manning and others (Hinshelwood and Manning 1979). Rooted in experiments with the hospital-based mental health services during and after the Second World War, they have spread slowly and unevenly in the community-based mental health services and beyond. From its inception, the therapeutic community sought to replace the traditional hierarchical structures of hospital management with a more democratically organized approach to care. This was an approach through which problems of individual and group functioning became the focus of concern for staff and residents, and one which blurred some of the accepted divisions between 'experts' and 'clients'.

This concern to develop an alternative to the established forms of residential management was promoted by a desire to exploit therapeutically all facets of the residential experience, in order to provide a means of enhancing individual functioning. The key to realizing this therapeutic exploitation was identified as one of 'caring through relationships'; a method crucially dependent on creating relationships stripped as far as possible of their institutional trappings and providing experiences of genuine concern and personal encounter.

The idea that it is through good experiences of personal relationships that individual growth and change takes place, has also played a part in the development of alternative communities. Such communities, like therapeutic communities, have questioned whether it is possible for such experiences to be provided through the traditional structures of family, work, and community in Britain. With visions of alternative forms of life style and society, they have been concerned to promote and develop alternatives to the family in its current form. Some have focused their concerns on disabled groups and, through voluntary organizations such as the Home Farm and Camp Hill Trusts in Britain, have tried to develop a communal way of life in which all are expected to participate according to their ability. The aim has been for disabled people to have the opportunity of experiencing activities which they are normally denied in our society. The assumptions on which these alternative communities are based explicitly challenge the notions of 'integration' and 'normalization' which are part of the vocabulary of community care for disabled groups. They do so because they question the capacity of wider society to provide such groups with anything but devalued and token participation.

Whether the provision of family-alternative care has led practitioners to develop existing institutional patterns or search for fresh approaches, it has raised common problems for all concerned in it. Four central problems are considered here: the development of family-alternative regimes; worker and resident relationships; contact with the family; and the management of transitions. The potential of this kind of care is then discussed.

Developing family-alternative regimes

By rejecting the option of developing regimes which attempt to replicate family life, residential workers in family-alternative units leave themselves with a considerable task: the selection and development of alternative regimes which provide positive residential experience. There are some well-established alternatives on which staff can draw, but there still remains an area of choice; an area shaped and constrained by the complex evidence available on residential outcomes, financial considerations, and wider policy issues. Once the choice is made, there are still considerable problems in actually developing the kind of regimes which reflect the goals and care philosophies that units claim to be pursuing.

In identifying the problems likely to confront staff in developing family-alternative regimes, the literature which has described the changes involved in the transformation of approved schools into community homes with education provides a rich source of material. Essentially, the conditions for this transformation were created by the provision of the Children and Young Persons Act 1969, which disbanded the approved school system and integrated the schools with local authority child care residential provision. In doing so, the Act reflected a belief that there exists a similarity between the needs of delinquent children and those of deprived children; the logic of this viewpoint was the provision of similar residential care for both groups. In the attempts which have been made to bring the regimes of former approved schools closer to those of children's homes, a number of common problems have emerged.

Two books which offer accounts and some analysis of these issues are Wills's *Spare the Child* (1971) and Cawson's more recent study of three community homes with education, *Community Homes: a Study of Residential Staff* (1978).

David Wills describes in his book some of the problems which emerged in changing the regime of the Cotswold Approved School into a therapeutic community for delinquent boys. The regime had been one which provided a traditional, disciplined training experience for delinquent boys. As a regime it was the product of a hierarchically structured organization in which all authority and responsibility was vested in the headmaster. This structure was based on what Wills describes as a punitive, authoritarian tradition of control embodied in a clear set of rules, prohibitions, and punishments; a system in which staff were graded, and residents were graded both by the staff and each other; a system in which relationships between staff and residents, and residents and residents, were conducted within a tight system of regulation and punishment.

When the decision was taken to change the residential experience the school offered to delinquent boys, the alternative-care model selected was that of a therapeutic community. As the discussion of the assumptions underlying this particular model suggests, it was one which differed fundamentally from the traditional approach of the school. Its perspective implied that residents and potential residents were not wicked youngsters who needed to be taught how to behave, rather they were 'unhappy, deprived persons who need care and healing', victims of society, and rejected by their own families. Inherent in this view was the notion that the custodial and punitive emphasis of the school's regime needed to be replaced by a 'community of stable concerned adults and delinquent children, where communication was uninhibited by artificial barriers' and where, through the growth of caring relationships, the children would learn to adopt new ways of behaviour through modelling themselves on the staff.

The structure of such a community was seen as evolving from the daily encounters between staff and residents, taking shape through the experience of adult–child relationships 'based on concern rather than control'. It was therefore a structure in which authority was a matter for each individual and was exercised through relationships of trust and openness, rather than a formally designated chain of command.

Wills describes the many difficulties encountered in translating into practice this radically different approach to residential living. His analysis suggests that many of these difficulties arose from the fact that the approach selected knocked away the structure of formal discipline, which was such a key part of the world of staff and residents. This discipline was to be replaced by nothing more tangible than an aspiration that open personal relationships would blossom. The great uncertainties and tensions generated by this change reflected the fact that staff were left to fall back on their own resources rather than a publicly recognized disciplinary framework. Wills suggests that many staff found this responsibility both frightening and exhausting, yet this was a process which could not be avoided. For in Wills's view, residential workers who are to provide the kind of residential experience inherent in the therapeutic community approach need to strip themselves of the protection of authoritarian staff roles, in order to exercise personal authority within caring relationships with residents.

This account suggests that residential workers developing alternative regimes face a major problem when they are working to change or modify an accepted tradition of care. In acknowledging this, they need to anticipate and work through the different demands likely to be made on themselves and residents, by the change; demands which not only question previous methods of working but also fundamental attitudes towards the residential experience itself. Wills's account suggests that some choices which are made can so transform a worker's role that the resultant stress and uncertainty may endanger successful change.

Cawson's study takes further this problem of initiating regimes which challenge well-established care traditions. In it she tried to measure some of the consequences for three former approved schools of becoming part of the local authority child care system. Cawson suggests that, as a result of this change, the homes reflected a mixture of at least three 'different institutional and professional traditions, from the penal system, the educational system, and the child care system' and that this mixture resulted in a more complex work situation for staff than that typical of other residential units and schools for children.

In tracing the consequences of this unique heritage for the staff of the schools Cawson noted that they all faced a common problem despite their individual differences in philosophy and regime: 'an organizational conflict between the new goals of parenting and treatment . . . and the traditional organizational educational and custodial goals which had been part of the old Approved School task' (Cawson 1978 : 3). The outcome of this conflict, in Cawson's view, is the predominance of the traditional school structure and the consequent constraints on those staff interested in developing the individualized, child-centred approach to care promoted as the major means of realizing a change in purpose for the schools.

Whilst Wills's analysis of the problems of developing alternative regimes emphasized the difficulties encountered by staff who retain traditional attitudes and responses, Cawson's analysis points to the consequence for staff of retaining organizational structures which reflect a traditional approach. Cawson demonstrates how workers' efforts to realize the kind of regime outlined in *Care and Treatment in a Planned Environment* (Advisory Council on Child Care 1970), that of 'an integrated provision of education care and treatment which would meet an individual child's needs' were frustrated by the structure of administrative and professional organization.

The lessons which can be drawn from these studies, and others, suggest that workers involved in developing regimes need to take into account both the attitudes established by previous care regimes and the organization of those regimes; for these can both limit and continue to influence the new regime.

Even if both these factors are worked with, staff may still find they are confronting problems in establishing an alternative regime, if that regime does not fit easily into the structure and expectation of the wider organization of which the unit is a part.

This facet of the problems of regime development has been particularly vividly documented in some of the accounts of the struggles to establish therapeutic community wards in psychiatric hospitals. The tensions generated by the development of a ward regime which challenged some of the traditional care assumptions of the larger institution often resulted in the isolation of therapeutic community wards and their staff within the hospital.

An interesting account of one such experience is Cooper's description of the problems encountered in attempting to establish an alternative residential facility for schizophrenics within a psychiatric hospital (Cooper 1970 : 96). Villa 21 was a unit in which staff and residents attempted to explore together the treatment implications of Laing's view of schizophrenia. This view, which suggests that schizophrenia may be the logical response of individuals to stressful situations, is also one which sees healing as dependent upon individuals being given the time and space to explore their problems. In attempting to create a community which encouraged and allowed for such individual 'voyages of discovery,' Cooper and his nursing colleagues found that its implementation challenged many basic hospital routines. In adopting a different stance to such issues as ward cleanliness, timetabled mealtimes, and patient-staff relationships, staff found themselves subject to outside pressures to conform to the expected and accepted care approaches.

Such experiences demonstrate how the successful development and establishment of alternative-care regimes may be highly dependent on their legitimation by the wider organization of which they are part. Where this legitimation is the green light for change, residential staff will be freed to work on the problems of the unit; where it is still negotiable, staff may find themselves spending time and energy justifying and protecting their venture.

Worker and resident relationships

Whilst the notion of 'parenting' is a complex one to translate into residential practice, it does provide some common basis from which residential workers can begin to work out, individually and collectively, how to relate to residents. Workers in family-alternative units have no equivalent idea on which to draw. Instead, most are faced with developing relationships with residents within the boundaries prescribed by the traditions of their unit's regime. In considering the problems this raises, one is struck by the division between those units which model themselves on established institutions and those which attempt to develop alternative modes of organization. In the first kind of unit, staff are faced with a variety of constraints on developing close relationships with residents; in the second kind, the problems arise from lack of such constraint. Both situations generate particular kinds of conflict and tension which shape and modify the style an individual worker will come to adopt.

Let us look first at those units structured on traditional lines. A caring style which has had, since the days of the nineteenth-century workhouses and asylums, a considerable influence on the practice of some residential staff has been nursing. This influence has stemmed from the fact that it offers an accepted and 'professional' mode of relating to dependent individuals, as well as a tried and established method of administering and organizing residential care. Yet, in the post-war period in Britain, this approach has come under increasing criticism and is now seen as inappropriate for most client groups in residential care. Its weakness has been identified by many commentators as lying in its prime concern with the physical functioning of individuals. They argue that this focus results in stress being placed on the dependance and disabilities of the individual residents. They also point out that this focus results in a method of organizing care in which the tasks needed to ensure physical comfort are the prime concern of the caretakers' efforts.

Oswin's accounts of the daily living experiences of groups of handicapped children in long-term care, vividly demonstrates the fragmented and confused encounters which this approach to caring provides for individual residents. The logic, from the workers' point of view, of regarding care as a series of tasks such as dressing, washing, toileting, and feeding, reduces the resident to a 'part' on a conveyor belt which is serviced in a routine fashion. As a result, staff and residents become locked in impersonal, and often silent, exchanges clearly outside the boundaries of ordinary human exchange (Oswin 1973).

In offering an explanation of why this style of caring has persisted, Menzies, Miller and Gwynne, and others have suggested that, in emphasizing social distance and depersonalizing physical caring tasks, it provides staff with some defences against the stress and anxiety inherent in caring for others. It also gives status and a visible routine to the work undertaken (Menzies 1960; Miller and Gwynne 1972). As the discussion of family-substitute care suggests, the pursuit of 'resident-oriented' practices can generate tensions which workers find difficult to negotiate. Nursing care which is 'institution-oriented' can protect staff from such conflict, yet experience suggests that in the long term protection can have a demoralizing effect on care staff.

One of the few written accounts of an attempt by a group of staff to move away from this style of caring can be found in Towell and Harries (Towell and Harries 1979 : 67).

The nurses who provided care for thirty-three elderly, mentally infirm women in the ward of a psychiatric hospital, became concerned to improve the care which they gave their residents. They asked themselves three questions: what do we spend our time doing? what difference does high and low staffing make to our activities? what is the difference between weekend and weekday routines? They provided the answers by recording their activities in detail over a trial period. The findings suggested a great deal of 'institution-orientated' activity, which increased rather than decreased with extra staff. These observations, together with an assessment of residential functioning, provided an agreed list of target problems on which to work in order to change the nature of worker–resident interaction. On the basis of a year's work, the nurses were able to identify improvements arising from their efforts including: relief of pressure on staff; increased activity of residents in caring for themselves; increased conversation between staff and residents; and a change in staff attitudes; 'seeing the patient as an object rather than a human being is, we hope, something of the past. It is also true that everyone has enjoyed looking at the patients in a different light from that of purely physical care' (Towell and Harries 1979 : 73). In other words, it was not just the residents who became involved more actively in ward life, there was a marked increase in staff interest and morale, as their work became less institution-oriented.

Faced with the problems of developing a satisfactory caring style, residential workers in traditional units may find their practice aspirations are at odds with the organization and staffing structures of their establishment. There is now considerable evidence (Gill 1974; Millham, Bullock, and Cherrett 1975; Cawson 1978) that in child care units organized on boarding school lines, there are likely to be considerable limitations placed on the kind of relationships that residential workers are able to establish with residents. In Cawson's study, mentioned earlier, it was suggested that, whatever the detailed differences in regimes, residential workers shared a common problem in realizing the child care element of their task. Whilst most staff recognized the importance of providing a good experience of adult care and concern for residents, they encountered considerable difficulties in establishing the kind of relationships which generated such an experience. Clear norms of behaviour had been established in all these units with regard to the classroom, yet in the daily living routine there appeared to be no equally clear model on which staff and residents could draw. Although care staff used family analogies in describing the kind of relationships they thought they should be establishing with boys, their practice did not reflect this ideal at all.

Cawson's analysis suggests that the reason for this gap between aspiration and practice can be traced to the problem of attempting to realize child care within a structure which has been shaped by the bureaucratic organization of a boarding school. The organizational framework conducive to the successful realization of teaching and training Cawson suggests, is in conflict with the exercise of individual responsibility needed to be a good house-parent. As a result:

'house-parents seemed to see themselves as they were defined; a stage in the bureaucratic process. No longer the caring adult who provided for the child's needs, they often felt reduced to being part of the machinery which filled in forms for the issue of clothing, or conveyed information to the seniors. Their responsibility was not towards the child but towards the Headmaster or Matron, by seeing that procedures were carried out in accordance to rules or policies.'   (Cawson 1978 : 66)

Two consequences of this restriction on individual caring initiatives were, first, that the child care task of workers was viewed as 'less professional' and therefore of a lower status than the educational tasks and, second, that both workers and residents recognized that the relationships which developed between them were shaped by a system much larger than any individual's personal interest or concern. Indeed, Cawson suggests that the resident–staff relationships which typify this kind of unit are in fact a complete reversal of the usual parent–child relationship.

'In the family, the affection develops first with the child as a dependent infant. Discipline and control are established later when the child's growing independence makes them necessary. Control is therefore established in the context of an already secure care relationship. The school situation reverses this procedure . . . but its practice of advising staff to be "firm, almost cold" at first and attempt to establish warmth only when the control relationship is secure.'   (Cawson 1978 : 168)

THERAPEUTIC COMMUNITIES

It is interesting that therapeutic communities evolved from attempts by residential workers to confront openly just the kind of influence organization structures had on their relationships with residents. As an alternative approach to both family care and traditional institutional approaches, these communities have tried to create structures which enhance, rather than undermine, intense, personal relationships between workers and residents. The rationale for this is that it is through caring relationships, stemming from genuine concern and regard, that residential communities can effect individual change.

The problem this approach to client–worker relationships raises for residential workers centres on the demands it makes on them to share themselves with others. As the discussion of the assumptions which underlie the therapeutic community suggests, this view of caring rests on a belief that residential communities can provide positive healing experiences, if all their members are prepared to share their feelings, perceptions, and needs and work together at the problems which emerge in living together. Residential workers in such communities are faced with dual expectations. On the one hand, they are expected as any other community member is, to 'open up' as individuals and share their feelings. At the same time they are expected, as staff, to hold on to the notion that the community exists to help its residents; to achieve this end, staff must provide a source of stability, on which residents can draw in testing out new attitudes and behaviours.

The 'style' which workers develop will reflect their attempts to balance these demands. In developing a 'style' in this way, each worker is likely to be confronted with particular problems relating to his use of authority in the therapeutic community. The lack of a hierarchical power structure based on either a family or traditional institutional model, throws each worker back on his or her own resources in negotiating the daily crises which are bound to occur in community living. In explaining their responses to these crises, workers are not encouraged to refer to the job 'expected of them'. Instead, the emphasis is on responsibility being vested in individuals who personally justify their actions both intellectually and emotionally.

This individual allocation of responsibility and authority raises difficult questions for workers about the distinction between 'professional' and 'personal' behaviour. In a residential unit, where workers are encouraged to avoid hiding behind formal roles, it may be difficult at times to maintain the traditional boundary between professional relationships and friendships, and this may increase feelings of vulnerability and uncertainty.

Yet there are some practitioners, such as Bettelheim, who insist that this dilemma should not be avoided. For if workers are to create residential communities which have a substantial impact on the behaviour and attitudes of their residents, they need to develop and use a deep, personal commitment to their work (Bettelheim 1974). If this commitment calls into question traditionally accepted boundaries then so much the better, as long as it is a commitment subjected to a shared intellectual scrutiny which ensures that residents are helped, rather than hindered, in their path of self-discovery.

Some family-alternative units have dealt with this issue of professional and friendship boundaries by viewing it as irrelevant to the achievement of their task. One example of this can be found in the work of the Arbours Association in London which was founded 'to give individuals who had been or could become mental patients the time, space, and encouragement to confront, rather than escape from their emotional, physical, and spiritual problems and to achieve a personal stance which was truly their own' (Berke 1979 : 118). In order to achieve this, a network of households has been established which provides a crisis centre and three long-stay communities each with seven to fourteen members. In these houses the traditional roles of 'staff' and 'patient' are not recognized. Instead, the emphasis is on the creation of a communal way of life which can provide support, when needed, for all its members.

Other examples can be found in those communities concerned to create self-sufficient alternatives to family and community life, which emphasize that members should demonstrate a willingness to share life experiences and skills, rather than present themselves as clients or professionals.

This questioning of the necessity for traditional staff and resident boundaries still leaves community members with the problems of creating and maintaining relationships through shared living which provide satisfying and positive experience for those involved. It leaves unanswered the question of how much can be given by any one individual, and for how long, before he or she becomes exhausted or 'burnt out' by the demands made on them.

The unit and the family

Inherent in the assumptions which inform the practice of most family alternative units are notions of what constitutes appropriate contact between residents and their family or friends. As the studies of Oswin and Miller and Gwynne indicate, units which base their care regimes on a hospital or 'warehousing' model, view family contact primarily in terms of what 'fits' the needs of the unit's routine rather than the expressed needs of residents and families. Set visiting hours, active discouragement of 'out of hours' contact, and exchanges with staff which are limited to reassurances about the resident's 'condition', all minimize disruption of the normal pattern of daily care (Oswin 1973; Miller and Gwynne 1972).

Units which model their organization and regime on the boarding school can also draw on an established pattern of family contact. Lambert and Millham in their study of British boarding school life suggest that an important part of the function of these institutions is the provision of an experience which weakens the individual's dependence on meeting his social and emotional needs through the family. This is reflected in deliberate limitation of contact with family during the school term and active discouragement of displays of homesickness (Lambert and Millham 1968).

Contact with families is also used in some units as a means of controlling and changing resident behaviour. Some family-alternative regimes view family contact as a privilege which has to be earned by the resident, and a privilege which can be withdrawn as a form of punishment. Such regimes do not consider such contact as a right or as a necessarily consistent feature of the individual's residential experience. Taylor's discussion of the care practices adopted in community homes with education suggests that this approach to family contact has become incorporated in some of the behavioural programmes used in these units. Alongside cigarettes and sweets, home leave is used as a 'back up reinforcer' for individual residents (Taylor, Lacey, and Bracken 1980).

The Phoenix House residential project which offers treatment for drug addicts in America and Britain uses family contact in a similar way. These highly structured and hierarchically organized alternative communities impose initial isolation on all new members. In Rosenthal's words:

'At the induction centre where all new members spend their first stage of residence, generally for three weeks to a month, even looking out of the window is discouraged. Isolation at this stage of membership acts to intensify commitment to the organisation and to prevent the intrusion of conflicting demands, for example from drug-using buddies or family members. The means for isolating new members of the group involve the establishment of new interactional territories, bounded by physical space which constitutes the drug-free social landscape, peopled by fellow members of the community who are committed to developing new behavioural and interactional patterns.'   (Jansen 1980 : 109)

This control of family contact in order to increase the therapeutic impact of a unit on its residents has been used in relation to a range of client groups. One of the most fully developed rationales for this approach in relation to the residential care of emotionally disturbed children can be found in Bettelheim's accounts of the work of the orthogenic school in Chicago.

In describing the family situations from which the school's residents have been drawn, Bettelheim emphasizes the 'pernicious interaction' which typically characterizes the relationships between parent and child, and which plays an important part in sustaining the fears lying at the root of the child's abnormal behaviour. In the face of this, the aim of the school is to physically separate resident and family and to provide an environment in which the resident can learn how to function more adequately. For, in Bettelheim's view, 'to be physically removed from whatever persons the child is afraid to learn about, takes some sting out of the fear of exploring' (Bettelheim 1950 : 127).

In order to maximize the use which a resident can make of this experience, the school has rules which set limits on ongoing family contact. The policy is one of 'coupling long-term treatment with rare home visits'. When home visits are sanctioned, they are arranged just a few weeks in advance on the basis of 'what seems best for the child'.

> 'Uncertainty about when the child will be available prevents the parent from simply postponing gratification, through the child, of his neurotic needs until the time of the next visit. The parents are not able to keep their neuroses in "deep-freeze" until their children come home. Restrictions of visits, control over presents that are intended to bribe or induce feelings of guilt, a censorship that prohibits letters containing criticisms of the child or warnings and admonitions about what he ought and ought not to do, and abso-lute protection of the child against his parents knowing how he misbehaves at school, all serve first to reduce, then to eliminate the child's and the parents' ability and need to act against each other.'   (Bettelheim 1950 : 491).

An important element in this strategy is the protection of those staff who are in closest emotional contact with the child from direct exchanges with parents. It is argued that this protection is needed to ensure the unhindered development of therapeutic relationships; parents with questions and criticisms are directed to staff members who are not working closely with their child.

The emphasis on family pathology which underlies this use of family contact, can also be traced in other residential communities. Those communities in Britain which base their work on R. D. Laing's view that mental illness can be seen as a way of coping with some forms of family life, seek to provide their members with an alternative to, and a protection from, family relationships.

What has been suggested here is that the problems raised for family-alternative units in relating to the family are complex. First, the models used in developing care regimes may prescribe particular patterns of contact and prohibit others. Workers need to be aware of the impact that these prescriptions have on the lives of residents as well as on their own practice. Lambert and Millham's study of boarding schools, shows how differently families experience this form of care. For those parents who choose and pay for a public school for their children the choice reflects 'the continuation of the family's already established pattern of sharing the physical care and some other aspects of the upbringing of the child with agencies outside the immediate family' (Lambert and Millham 1968). In contrast, those parents and children involved in the state's various equivalents of boarding school tend to experience them as a drastic interruption of the established pattern of child care and family life. Such differences in the relationship of family life to particular residential solutions must have consequences for the individual's reactions to and use of the residential experience.

Second, there is strong evidence that workers in some kinds of family-alternative unit are encouraged to view the issue of family contact as just a part of more important concerns such as the mainte-nance of routine, discipline, and control within the unit itself. When this is the case, then issues are raised about resident and family rights in relation to residential regimes.

Finally, in considering this problem one becomes aware of a very uncertain area in which some workers are attempting to use residen-tial units to retain a balance between individual well-being and family involvement. This is an area where it is difficult to specify with any precision the conditions under which the limitation of resident and family contact can be therapeutically justified, and workers attempt-ing to do so are likely to find themselves faced with conflicting pressures.

Managing transitions

A criticism which is often made of family-alternative regimes is that they create problems for the individual resident who leaves to rejoin the outside world. The ground for this criticism is that the routine of many family-alternative regimes tends to promote social interaction which differs markedly from the kind of behaviour appropriate to the world outside the unit. Whereas family-substitute units and family-support units are concerned to incorporate into their programmes family-type routines and expectations, family-alternative regimes can tend to be immune from such concerns.

A great deal has been written about the problem faced by both residents and workers in tackling the management of transition from family-alternative units to the community. Studies in the 1960s of the effects of 'institutionalization' on mentally disabled people who had spent considerable periods in psychiatric hospitals (Barton 1976; Morris 1969; Wing and Brown 1970) are a case in point. These studies suggested that the interaction which typified large, medically-oriented regimes, resulted in the handicapping loss of social skills in patients. In learning to survive and make their life in these institutions, individuals had to abandon the rules and roles which applied in the outside world.

While the effects of this type of experience will vary according to both the regime of the unit and the length of time an individual spends in it, it is a feature of residential solutions which is particularly apparent in regimes that deliberately offer alternatives to family and community life.

Another facet to this problem of managing transition is that some of the difficulties which individual residents have are the direct consequence of factors in their home environment. Moving from a residential unit back into that environment may trigger those difficulties regardless of any changes in individual attitude and behaviour that may have taken place during the period of residence in a unit. While those working in family-support units are concerned, as the next chapter will describe, to focus on the home environment as part of the residential programme, this is unlikely to be a direct concern of those working in family-alternative units. Instead, in focusing on the behaviour of the individual resident, such units are likely to regard the home environment much more as 'background information' on the individual, rather than as a matter for active intervention on their part. Those alternative units which stress the pathological influence of the home environment on the individual will view the residential experience as a means of counteracting some of the consequences of this pathology, so that the individual emerges strong enough either to seek an alternative to family life, or able enough to withstand the onslaught which a return to the family will bring. Some therapeutic communities, for example, have developed programmes which they hope will impart the skills necessary to enable individuals to work at family and relationship difficulties on their return home.

TRANSITIONAL PROGRAMMES

In tackling the problems of managing transitions, which are caused by both the influence of the regime on the individual resident and the impact of returning to adverse home and community circumstances, staff in family-alternative units appear to have developed two main strategies. The first is the creation of special transitional programmes to help residents with re-entry into the outside world. The second is the creation of long-term alternatives to family and community life through communal living situations linked to the original unit.

The transitional programmes which have been developed have tended to be based on the rehabilitative ideas outlined in more detail in chapter six. Their focus has been on re-activating those areas of social functioning which the residential experience has left to wither, by simulating the kind of conditions residents are likely to have to cope with on leaving the unit. The view is that, by gradually increasing these new demands, the resident's transition from the unit to the outside world will be eased as confidence in his ability to cope grows.

Examples of such programmes abound. They can be found in the attempts by some units catering for young people to create a hostel or flat situation, linked to the original home. Here residents, with decreasing amounts of support from staff, can learn to budget, cook, and manage independent living. Similarly, some hostels for the mentally ill and mentally handicapped have a flat attached to the unit to which residents are transferred when they have reached the stage of discharge into the community. This step in a resident's career is often marked by a physical separation from the regime of which he or she has been a part.

Foster, in an interesting account of the introduction of a transitional programme into a residential unit for drug addicts, shows how the first step in introducing the programme was to set a time limit of nine months on the length of residence in the unit; 'this was not because ex-addicts only require nine months of psychotherapeutic help, but because to offer a longer time in residential treatment hinders their rehabilitation' (Hinshelwood and Manning 1979:277). In addition, residents were encouraged to maintain links with the outside world during their stay and after their 'treatment period' there was the possibility of staying a further three months in a flat at the top of the house in which the unit was housed. This period was designated as a period of 're-entry' during which individuals were expected to make arrangements for their future and participate in a weekly group with others who had recently returned to the community.

Transitional programmes introduce a stage into the residential experience during which residents both increase their separation from the regime of the unit as well as their contact with the world to which they are returning. In order to ensure that this is an experience which does serve as a bridge between the unit and the outside world, workers need to limit the scope and nature of their own involvement in the lives of those residents who are making the transition. This can be very taxing for staff who have established relationships with residents which are based on a considerable degree of involvement in and concern about their daily lives. Yet unless this pattern is broken, it may be difficult for residents to develop sufficient confidence and autonomy to manage successfully their transition from the residential unit to the outside world.

LONG-TERM ALTERNATIVES

Not all residents of family-alternative units re-enter the worlds of family and community life. Some residents remain in units through design rather than through lack of any viable alternative. There are units which aim to provide alternative communal living for as long as residents need it. Others offer residents the possibility of remaining in the unit by changing their role. In those units where the experience of being a resident is seen as enhancing an individual's potential as a helper, residents may be offered the opportunity to demonstrate this potential. In the Phoenix House Communities, for example, this is an established step in the total care programme offered. Here, a rise in position in the hierarchy of the organization is earned as an individual moves successfully through the stages of the programme.

'Positions within the status and authority hierarchy at Phoenix House are allocated on the basis of conduct within the community.

The absence of traditional staff/patient dichotomy enables any member, regardless of his lack of extrinsic credentials, to rise high within the hierarchy if his performance warrants it.'

(Jansen 1980 : 108)

For some short-term units, however, there are considerable difficulties in managing transition because there are few alternatives for residents to move into. This can arise because residents are competing with other groups for scarce resources or because the experience of intensive communal living poses difficulties for those transferring to situations where they are expected to manage alone. It is as a result of experiencing these problems that some units have developed small long-term alternative communities which can be offered to residents leaving the main unit. By these means individuals can continue to experience group support, albeit in a less intense form, and maintain their links with the unit. Group homes and Arbours-style communities are examples of this solution.

In some family-alternative units the problems staff face in managing transitions relate to the residential care system itself. A number of units have specialist functions which are directed at transferring residents to other residential units. Observation and Assessment Centres for children and young people, for example, were created to provide a detailed analysis of a resident's needs in order to facilitate placement in a suitable residential setting. Taylor and his colleagues amongst others suggest that in practice they have faced difficulties in realizing this function and, as a result, have taken on the role of 'warehousing' children who have presented problems for other parts of residential and community services (Taylor, Lacey, and Bracken 1980). Similarly, staff in assessment units for other client groups, such as the elderly, may find that when residents appear to require substantial care, there are few residential alternatives to which they can be transferred. When this is the case, staff face the same dilemma; if they provide ongoing care themselves, they change the intended function of their unit.

There are, of course, those units which specialize in providing 'safe' or 'secure' accommodation for individuals who have not been contained in other residential and community situations. There is a great deal of literature on the kind of circumstances which surround the use of these kinds of units in the child care services. The research undertaken by Millham and his colleages (1978) and Cawson and Martell

(1979) has established that it is the consequence of residential care, rather than the individual's background, which play the greatest part in effecting the transition of a child from ordinary residential care to a secure unit. This being the case, the questions residential workers must ask themselves are considerable. How far can the development of this kind of specialist unit be justified on the grounds of individual resident need? How far does it reflect the problems of the residential care system itself?

The potential of family-alternative care

In broad terms it can be said that, potentially, family-alternative care widens the range of experiences that individuals can derive from residential communities. What is more, in some instances it can widen the range of alternatives to the nuclear family. As has been seen, however, a widening of choice does not ensure an increase in beneficial outcome for workers or residents.

In their discussions of the radical possibilities of this kind of residential unit for children, Lee and Pithers suggest that the challenge such units face lies in providing a communal way of life which, in offering an alternative experience, also confronts the reality of the outside world with which the children will have to deal. They argue that if they do not meet the challenge they may burden their residents: 'It is not helpful to a person who has to add to the unremitting hostility of the outside world the fact of having been brought up in an alternative way' (Brake and Bailey 1980 : 112).

The suggestion here is that, in order to maximize the positive potential of family alternative care, residential workers need to balance the demands of the unit's regime against the demands of the world to which residents are likely to return. They must not just serve the long-term interests of residents, but also ensure the survival of the unit.

It is worth reflecting here on the written experience of a group of local authority residential workers in a project based in Harlesden in the mid-1970s (Dharamsi *et al.* 1979).

The workers involved in this project explicitly rejected the idea of setting up a family group home on the grounds that: 'in the very difficult world of residential care, with few answers agreed, and many needs not being properly met, an alternative model was worth trying'.

The model they evolved was based on the belief that: 'a group of adults can provide effective care for a group of children and for each other without becoming parental figures, and without different statuses such that one, or a few, members of the group are regarded always as more important or as having more power or authority than the others.'

In attempting to realize this aim, they did not construct walls around their unit but attempted to use it as a community resource for others besides residents and staff; for use as 'a place where people can have a chance and help if they want in doing so, to sort out and make the choices they are faced with'.

In the ups and downs of life with a deprived and troubled group of young people, both residing in and visiting the unit, a recurring issue for staff was one of explaining their approach and negotiating its consequences both with their employing organization and the surrounding community. The structure of the staff group appeared to raise considerable difficulties for a local authority social services department, which was itself organized in a traditional, hierarchical manner. The absence of a head-of-home, or team leader, who took overall responsibility for the unit's work, was continuously questioned and criticized by departmental managers. In addition, the visibility of the project and the behaviour of the young people it catered for, led to complaints from the local community and police which the workers felt were seen as evidence of the team's failure to maintain adequate control and standards of conduct. A picture emerges of staff being unable to convince significant others of the merits of the approach they had chosen to adopt and in consequence finding themselves isolated in implementing their alternative model.

Realizing the full potential of any family-alternative unit depends on two main processes. First, workers need to recognize explicitly how the experience which their unit offers to residents is shaped by the choices they make about the unit's regime and organizational structure. Second, both staff and residents, need to be aware of the likely impact of external expectations on their way of life in the unit. In negotiating both of these, those involved in residential care will be confronted by wider constraints, which may limit their attempts to innovate. Millham and his colleagues suggest that in Britain 'our institutional heritage, both in thought and provision has limited the exploration of alternatives while the ever-increasing tasks of residential facilities inhibit experiment' (Tutt 1978).

Summary

Family-alternative care takes a variety of forms. The current range share an assumption that in certain circumstances there are negative aspects to family life. It is the stress put on this assumption which differentiates this type of care from either family-substitute or family-supplement care. Many family-alternative units have regimes which have adapted traditional organizational models such as schools, hospitals, and prisons, whilst others have explicitly sought to reject these and experiment with alternative organizational structures.

A number of problems faced by staff in family-alternative units relate to the choices which have been made in developing a particular regime, for such choices can call for particular attitudes and care practices which may be difficult for staff to realize. This can also have consequences for the employing organization or surrounding community with which staff will need to negotiate.

The choice of regime also has direct implications for the kind of relationships which develop between workers and residents. Whereas traditional units tend to place limits on the development of intense relationships between staff and residents, some alternative units actively encourage them. In both situations staff may face uncertainties and tensions and the style of caring each individual develops is likely to reflect the way in which he or she has balanced regime demands.

Because of the initial stance towards the family typifying this kind of unit, there is often an impetus to limit rather than encourage family contact. Some units use themselves deliberately as a means of breaking 'unhealthy' family ties; others see family contact as a way of rewarding residents' participation in the unit's programme; others concentrate their efforts on changing the individual resident in the belief that this will enable him, or her, to cope more effectively in the future with the family. Whatever approach is adopted, it raises questions about residents' rights as well as professional assessment.

Finally, the management of transition from a family-alternative unit generates particular difficulties for staff and residents. The regimes of some units may handicap residents when the time comes for them to live a more independent life and for this reason a number of units have developed transitional programmes to reactivate the individual's capacity and motivation for community living. Some family alternative units have developed specialist functions in relation to the residential care system, and resident transition may therefore prove difficult because of a lack of other care resources, or because entry into a specialist unit results in residents gaining a reputation for difficult behaviour. Those family-alternative units which seek to provide a radically different communal living experience may need to develop further residential resources in order to ensure that residents are able to maintain a life style they feel they can benefit from.

While family-alternative care plays a major part in current residential provision, there are still considerable problems to be faced by workers who are interested in exploring its full potential. Doubt has been thrown on the benefit to residents of some traditional regimes, where it appears impossible to develop the kind of relationships essential to a social work approach. On the other hand, there seem to be limits on innovation with alternative regimes. These limits appear to derive from traditional attitudes, financial considerations, and the current style of management support.

5

Family-supplement care

The idea that state residential care can be used in some circumstances to supplement and support family care is a relatively recent development. It has emerged from the increased emphasis in social work over the last thirty years on the notions of prevention and community care.

Prevention has been described as a way of identifying and responding to individual and family problems at an early enough stage to prevent breakdown and the use of long-term residential care. Effective prevention has been shown to be dependent on social workers being able to call on a range of resources as well as their own professional skills. Some of these resources have been based in residential units. Day care, holiday care, and assessment of individual functioning have increasingly drawn on both residential workers and the amenities of residential establishments. Where preventive programmes have been developed in this way, the aim appears to have been to integrate residential care with other community-based resources, in order to reinforce the efforts of families to continue to provide social care for dependent members.

Alongside this, ideas about community care have echoed the concern to keep dependent and deviant individuals in their own communities and families for as long as possible. Effective community care has been seen as a way of interweaving state welfare provision with the care networks of families, friends, and neighbours in order to delay or avoid the removal of individuals from their home environment to residential alternatives. As such, it has been promoted as a viable, long-term alternative to the large-scale residential institutions which have comprised the traditional state response to such groups as the mentally disabled, the physically handicapped, and juvenile offenders. As a strategy, community care has been seen as meeting the needs of a range of client groups and their families and as taking a wide variety of forms. Whilst community care programmes vary in the emphasis they place on the use of residential units as a means of supporting and servicing families and the local community, most have identified residential provision as an essential element in their structure. For example, Bayley's discussion of the kind of community care provision which would be responsive to the needs of families providing care for severely mentally handicapped relatives, gives a central role to small locally-based hostels as a means of providing specialist advice and ongoing support (Bayley 1973).

While these notions of prevention and community care have arisen in part from a concern to avoid the use of large-scale, long-term residential solutions, those interested in developing both these strategies argue for the retention of residential resources in a different form. Essentially they suggest that small residential units based in, and serving, local communities can offer a flexible way of supporting families with dependent members in periods of crisis by offering specialist advice and practical assistance and by regularly supplementing existing care networks. Such residential units are seen as having a potential as a unique, focused, and time-limited means of intervening in family situations in order to enhance individual and family functioning. This approach contrasts sharply with the traditional view that residential care is a resource to be offered as a substitute for, or alternative to, family care, and that its use is dependent on the removal of an individual from the community.

A substantial amount has now been written about this way of using residential care, but it is still difficult to find written accounts of units which are operating along these lines. This is disappointing because the problems being encountered in realizing this vision of residential intervention are important for residential workers to consider. After all, residential care which is directed at supporting and supplementing family care is a logical extension of social work. It 'fits' as a distinctly social work approach to managing and using residential resources and challenges a number of the traditions which have developed within residential care. It suggests that residential solutions have a positive potential as intensive, focused forms of social intervention, rather than the negative one of being 'containers' or 'dustbins' for the unwanted. It questions the view of the pessimists that the therapeutic potential of residential care is limited in that its use must necessarily confirm individual and family pathology.

Before looking at the problems raised for workers trying to implement family-supplement care, it is important to consider the assumptions which have informed the development of this kind of approach.

In looking across the current range of residential units in Britain where an attempt is being made to use resources as a means of supporting and supplementing family care, one can identify three major types. The first is the unit which attempts to work with the entire family by offering accommodation and intensive support for a limited period. The second type of unit offers short-term residential care for one family member on the basis that it will enhance both individual and family functioning in the long term. The third type provides a residential resource for a number of families with dependent members on the basis that they will share care for as long as is necessary with the family.

Rehabilitating the family as a unit

The use of residential care for entire families, in order to improve their chances of survival as a unit, has had limited application in Britain. Essentially, it has been restricted to families with young children whose circumstances include actual or impending homelessness, large debts and a low income, as well as personal and interpersonal difficulties of various kinds.

The rationale on which residential work with such families is based, reflects several strands of the debate on family responsibility outlined in chapter two. Some workers favour a medical analogy in which some families are seen as 'sick' with symptoms apparent in the social and psychological difficulties they have. In terms of this analogy the residential unit can offer an asylum – a chance to convalesce, and regain health before re-entering the community.

Other workers emphasize the training or education which some deprived families need in order to cope successfully with the problems of living. They focus on the lack of parenting and household management skills shown by the mothers (in particular) and also the fathers in these families. They see residential units as a means of transmitting these skills in order to enhance family functioning.

Some workers draw heavily on ideas derived from family therapy. For them, residential units can provide a way of undertaking intensive therapeutic work with a family directed at increasing the self-esteem and confidence of family members in order to strengthen their problem-solving abilities in a variety of personal and social situations.

Such assumptions reflect perhaps little more than the range of current perspectives which are part of social work practice with similar families in the community. However, it is far from clear on what grounds it is possible to distinguish between families who can survive with the help of social work support and families whose circumstances are such that residential support is additionally required. Since family supplement units emerged in the light of the post-war debates about family life and problem families, they have operated in a rather grey area where it is difficult to determine exactly the mix of social and psychological factors which indicate the viability of residential intervention in family life.

The Seebohm Report, looking at this area in the mid-1960s, argued that it was possible to distinguish between the needs of families who were essentially homeless and those who needed 'special residential care'. They described the latter as a group whose circumstances were such that they could benefit from:

> 'rehabilitation or recuperative units of various kinds which take a family (including the husband where there is one) for a temporary period and provide them with accommodation, respite and support and any necessary training, to give them a reasonable chance of being able to manage on their own again if necessary with help from the personal social services.'

The suggestion here seemed to be that it was a history of recurring or 'chronic' difficulties which marked out families who could benefit from this kind of residential solution. In this case, family units are clearly seen as a final option, a resource only to be used when families have clearly failed to manage their own affairs. In a society where the predominant view is still that a 'healthy' family is one which draws on its own resources and retains maximum independence from state help, residential units which offer some families a 'respite' from the consequences of their failures are likely to be viewed with considerable ambivalence. The logic of offering such families a 'second chance' is likely to find only limited approval and, whatever assumptions inform the practice of residential workers in this field, they are bound to find the therapeutic rationale of their work questioned by other professionals and the community at large.

Rehabilitating the individual

The main task undertaken in the second type of unit is also one of rehabilitation – but here the emphasis is not on working with the entire family, but on improving the social functioning of an individual family member, in order to resettle or re-establish them in the family.

The notion of individual rehabilitation has its roots in medical practice where it is defined as a treatment process designed to restore the functioning of handicapped individuals. While some residential units do provide care for individuals whose handicaps are a direct consequence of organic disease or accident, the use of the concept of rehabilitation in residential work has not been confined just to this particular group. As Bean points out, the notion of rehabilitation has been applied widely in the field of social intervention to describe professional and policy responses to a range of social and personal problems. Where it has been applied, it has not been based on an 'organic' explanation of these problems, but has been drawn instead on an analogy between behaviour and organic disease (Bean 1976).

Residential workers and others have used this analogy in describing the personal and social problems encountered by some individuals as stemming from their inability to function 'normally'. Whether these inabilities are the result of social or personal deprivation, or disadvantage, they are taken by the worker to be handicaps which are impairing individual performance.

Residential units which operate on this basis offer a time-limited, intensive residential experience designed to focus on specific areas of handicap in order to improve and maintain an individual's capacity to cope with life. The areas focused on will vary depending on staff orientations and the client group, but underlying this approach is the assumption that the unit's aim is to effect the kind of personal change which will enable the individual to function more effectively in the community. In this kind of unit one of the key measures of 'more effective functioning' is the increased ability of individuals to settle into family life. Thus, while the individual's capacities are spotlighted, they are continuously related to the demands likely to be made on them by the family, as well as the world of work and leisure.

It is this concern with the relationship between the individual and the family which distinguishes the rehabilitative approach of family-supplement care from the rehabilitative approach adopted in those units described in chapter four as 'alternative communities'. Although the staff in both kinds of unit may well locate the reasons for some individual difficulties within family relationships, family-supplement units will attempt to work with these relationships in devising rehabilitation programmes for individual residents.

Sharing care with the family

The third type of unit which aims to support the family and supplement its care, has emerged from the belief that community-based residential units serving a defined area can offer a range of resources to families who are involved in the ongoing care of dependent members. This idea has not only been promoted as part of a strategy to avoid taking children into long-term care, but has also played a prominent part in discussions about the community care of mentally and physically disabled adults.

Bayley's study of a group of families providing care for their mentally handicapped relatives offers one of the most comprehensive rationales for developing this form of residential care for a specific client group. From his observations of the daily routines established in families who were caring for profoundly handicapped relatives, Bayley identified several points at which families could have used, to beneficial effect, supplementary help of a practical and advisory kind. A great deal of this help – aids and adaptations; holiday relief; day or night care; advice on handling particular forms of behaviour – could, he suggested, be offered from small, locally-based hostels, with specialist staff trained to share their knowledge and skills with the families. Interlocking with patterns of family care in this way offers a basis, in Bayley's view, for a more individualized and sensitive response to the needs of families and their dependants. Residential workers in such units he suggests would have to focus their skills on the family as a unit, meshing their resources with the 'structure of coping' already established by the family and taking over the major responsibility for care at periods when it would provide maximum benefit to the family caretakers (Bayley 1973).

The assumption here is that the residential unit should not confine itself to offering residential care for limited periods, but should also develop, in response to demonstrated need, other services such as day care, specialist advice on welfare benefits, and training in care techniques. In other words, the unit should be a community resource offering residential care as just a part of its response to families prepared to take continuing responsibility for their dependants.

All three types of unit, then, have evolved from a concern to use residential provision in a more flexible way, in order to supplement family care rather than replace it. This concern is based on the assumption that it is possible to use a residential experience as a means of improving the way in which families, their individual members, or both, cope with life in the wider community. It also assumes that residential care can enhance individual and family functioning in a way which prevents disintegration and increases the possibility of future independence. This emphasis on focused intervention as a means of engendering change is one which harmonizes the use of residential care most clearly with the stated aims of social work intervention. It promotes a view of the residential worker as an individual exercising the methods and skills of social work within an intensive therapeutic environment.

In practice, few units have yet realized this potential. Staff attempting to operate this form of residential intervention have found themselves facing considerable common difficulties. Four of these have been selected here for detailed consideration.

Problems of referral

When there is a tradition built into the use of residential care that it is a 'last resort', staff in residential units who are promoting the idea that they can be used before that point is reached, will find themselves facing problems in relation to referrals. Essentially the issue is one of timing. If residential care is to be used as a focused form of intervention, directed at improving the way in which individuals and families support themselves in the long term, its relevance needs to be considered at a point in individual and family situations where there is a chance of success. The social workers most likely to be alerted to, or involved with, such situations will not be residential workers. They are more likely to be fieldwork social workers whose use of residential solutions will depend on their understanding and experience of what they most typically offer. Family support units are not 'typical' and so the chances are that there will be significant differences of view between their staffs and fieldworkers about what constitutes an 'appropriate referral'. These differences can have a profound effect on the tasks which residential staff are able to undertake, as the assumptions on which these units have developed include the active involvement of unit staff at an early stage in the referral process. The work undertaken by this kind of unit is dependent on a detailed assessment of the situation which led to referral and the early development of a shared view of the problems which need to be worked with. In situations where whole families are involved, there is a built-in expectation that, to be effective, the unit's approach must be firmly grounded in the family's own view of its needs and difficulties. The realization of this approach is dependent either on the establishment of firmer patterns of co-operation between residential workers and their fieldwork colleagues, or a recognition of the need for a shift in the existing allocation of responsibilities between fieldworkers and those residential workers offering this particular form of care.

In addition, this active stance by residential workers to the referral and assessment process includes the real possibility that when the staff of a unit feel they have little to offer in a situation then they can refuse to accept an individual or family into their care. While residential workers may begin to resolve successfully some of their initial problems about involvement in referrals and assessment, they are likely to encounter much more resistance among their colleagues to the notion that they can exercise a right to refuse admission. Arguing for a limited and specific use of a residential unit, rather than accepting its use as a 'hold-all' for a variety of problems, challenges our residential care traditions. Residential workers who are identified with this challenge are likely to find themselves accused of being too 'exclusive'; of taking the 'easy' cases and leaving the 'difficult ones' for other units; and of not facing the 'realities' which are presented daily to the residential services. Faced with this kind of criticism, and working in a unit which may not be filled to capacity, workers are likely to feel isolated and guilty about 'wasting' an expensive resource. If they resolve these feelings by agreeing to admit what they consider to be 'inappropriate' referrals, they may well find themselves in a relatively short time having to abandon the idea that they can use their unit for the kind of short-term support work which they originally envisaged.

One of the few written accounts by a group of residential workers who were confronted by this problem is given in the book referred to in chapter four about a residential and community work project set up in the early 1970s to act as a locally-based resource in a deprived inner-city area. The initial aim of the residential workers employed by this project was to provide a service for young people whose difficulties, 'might fairly reflect, in an aggravated form perhaps, the general problems that can arise between parents and children in the period of adolescence' (Dharamsi *et al.* 1979 : 244). This service was planned as a short-stay hostel in two ordinary local houses staffed by a team of workers who would work from this base with both residents and their parents towards an agreed return home. Very quickly the workers realized that the group of young people being referred to them at the project did not fit their expectations. They were a group who had not only experienced long-standing difficulties with their families but had also been 'in touch with the services over many years, had been the round of other institutions and were presenting the existing resources with pressures they felt unable to cope with' (Dharamsi *et al.* 1979 : 245). Workers accepted some of these referrals and in doing so found they had to abandon their original objectives. The offer of a short period of care, could not, in the staff's view, repair the 'deep-seated damage' which residents had experienced and child–parent contact was usually too tenuous to provide a realistic focus for work. The unit, in deciding to offer something to this group of young people, adopted an approach which aimed to provide an alternative to, not a support for, family networks. Working on the basis that their residents were individuals who needed to work at, and though, relationships with adults in order to increase their chances of coping with adult life, they tried to use the houses and their own skills to provide opportunities for this. In addition, they attempted to develop the unit as an alternative resource for other young people who were part of the resident's local friendship networks and who shared similar difficulties.

While the needs of the client group will vary, this problem of referral is likely to be experienced by all units attempting to provide care designed to supplement and support family care. At the outset the unit, whatever its stated aims, will be viewed by others in the care system as an extra resource to house clients who are presenting problems to the existing residential and community services. There is a likelihood that such clients will have reached a stage in their lives when work focused on supporting and sustaining the family is no longer appropriate and therefore the unit's response to these referrals will have a decisive effect on its chances of developing a family support service.

This is a problem which is not easily resolved in situations of scarce resources and heavy demand. It emerges because the approach to referrals inherent in a family-support model of residential care is one which breaks so markedly with existing tradition and priorities in the service. When such breaks are being pioneered by isolated units, then these units appear to be more likely to fail than to succeed in their objectives, and staff are left feeling defeated; if they succeed, staff may find themselves frustrated by the under-use of a specialist resource.

Engaging the family

As has already been suggested, the assumptions which underlie this particular form of residential care emphasize the need for residential workers to take into active consideration the context in which the problems a resident brings to the unit have emerged. The stress placed on this will vary according to the client's situation and the orientation of the staff team, but it will always be a factor that influences the unit's task and places unique demands on residents, workers, and families.

In the first place, the basis on which these three parties relate will differ considerably from that in either family-substitute care or family-alternative care. In these latter cases residential workers are offering care to replace that which the family cannot or will not provide. In family-support units the worker is concerned not to replace family care, but to offer an experience through which a planned engagement with some of the difficulties arising from stressful family situations is possible. These difficulties are likely to include the quality of family relationships, individual attitudes and behaviours, and the availability of practical resources. The 'mix' will reflect the circumstances which have led to intervention in the first place, but the direction residential workers take will be one which is explicitly aimed at relating the learning experiences encountered in the unit to the situation to which the residents are returning.

It is because of this that 'engaging the family' in the residential experience becomes a particularly crucial problem for workers in this type of unit. To achieve their aims they need to work with the feelings generated by admission to the unit as part of the rehabilitative process. Kelly, in his account of the work of a specialist Richmond Fellowship Unit for families, comments on the fact that new families entering the unit appear to fear that they are going to be blamed for their situation and it is only as they begin to trust those in the unit that 'defences are lowered and the feelings of guilt, blame, helplessness, and failure can be shared' (Jansen 1980 : 153). The workers in this establishment see this sharing as the beginning of their attempt to work with families in trouble towards goals which have been jointly established on admission to the unit.

The focused, time-limited nature of this work relies on a structured use of the residential experience and its constant review in the light of staff and resident experience. Some workers in this type of unit have used contracts with residents, families, or both, as a means of achieving this kind of structure and actively involving all the parties concerned in planned change. This does no more than extend the use of a technique employed in other areas of social work practice. Some units use it at the initial point of contact, making it an essential part of the admission process. Others use it after an initial period of assessment, to clarify the objectives that staff, resident, and families are working towards.

Implicit in the approach of family-support units is that changes in family attitudes and behaviour may be as, if not more, important as changes in the attitude, behaviour, and functioning of an individual resident. At times the workers' skills will be engaged in working with all parties in the situation and success in initiating change will be dependent on the ability of both residents and families to use the opportunities offered.

It is obvious that workers operating in this kind of unit will be called on to develop and employ a wide range of skills with individuals and groups, as well as a willingness to relate to families as both clients and co-workers. In units which are attempting to engage with families in care-sharing, in ways similar to those outlined by Michael Bayley

(1973) and the Jay Report, this raises issues about family engagement which break totally new ground in residential care. Care-sharing places demands on residential workers to be not only 'experts' on whom families can draw, but also to be prepared to learn from and work closely with families on a variety of tasks. This approach calls for the 'opening up' of residential units so that families feel able to take part in the daily care of their own relatives and other residents and feel easy in doing so. An example of one unit attempting to achieve this is Field End House, a residential unit in London for children with multiple handicaps, offering long-term care, short-term care and day-care to a group of local children (McCormack 1979 : 201). Admission to the unit is conditional on parental involvement. Family members are expected to share as much in the care of their relatives as they can, working alone or with staff in doing so. Apart from this share in direct care, parents are also involved in the management of the unit, sharing with staff in policy decisions which affect the unit's approach and direction.

Engaging families in residential situations of this kind opens up an uncertain territory for residential workers and managers to explore. It increases the visibility of residential workers' practice and attitudes and in doing so it encourages the questioning of their effectiveness and direction. It demands that the task workers are undertaking is extended to take in not only circumstances arising in the unit but also circumstances arising in the family home. It suggests that techniques and solutions used in the residential situation should be such that they can be transferred and tested in the home situation. In contrast with other approaches it makes the achievements of residential work dependent on the successful engagement of the family in tackling problems.

Problems of transition

The ultimate test of residential units which aim to supplement and support the family is their success in managing the transition of individuals from the unit back into family life. For those establishments pursuing a rehabilitative programme with their residents, resettlement in the community will be seen as the final stage in a process which has succeeded in improving individual and family functioning. For those establishments pursuing the idea of care-sharing it will be the smooth transition between staff and family care within the unit, and between the unit and the home, which will demonstrate the achievement of a structure of caring which meets individual and family needs.

The problems staff face in working towards successful transitions appear to stem from two main sources: first, the effects of the residential experience itself and, second, changes in the family situation.

A residential experience which is used to focus on particular difficulties in behaviour, attitudes, and personal relationships, cannot guarantee an outcome of improved individual functioning or the strengthening of the family unit. It can, instead, reveal the limits of an individual capacity for change and so call into question the aim of resettling him or her with the family. Families who enter it may use the experience to decide that there are more reasons for abandoning their life together than there are for continuing it. Some families may experience such relief when an individual member enters care, that they may decide they cannot return to carrying the main responsibility for caring.

When outcomes like this occur as a result of an admission to care, residential workers are faced with situations which are familiar to social workers in other settings. They are working with individuals and families who have reached the limits of coping and are in crisis about their future. However, residential workers face these situations from a base which can provide twenty-four hour, seven-day-a-week care; a base which can be used as an alternative to family life and which can, therefore, 'hold' the problem for considerable periods. The dilemma thrown up for workers by this is a very acute one. In the absence of alternative care in the community, or in the presence of an apparent inability to manage re-settlement, it is difficult to withdraw the unit's facilities on the grounds that it can no longer work towards family support. Yet if those facilities are not withdrawn, the unit is likely to find itself holding residents to the extent that its main task with them shifts from that of time-limited intervention to that of longer term care. As a result, the emphasis on transition will be lost and the residential programmes will increasingly reflect this.

Other changes in the circumstances of individuals and families can take place which are not directly connected with the experience of admission to a family-support unit. Loss of employment; a change in the size and type of the family's accommodation; the death or illness of the family caretaker; increased dependency of another family member – these and other changes can generate problems in managing successful transitions from the unit to the community. Residential staff may have provided an experience which has enhanced both individual and family functioning, but if there is not a viable home base for the resettlement of a resident then their efforts cannot be put to the test. Whatever the original motivation of a family to share the care of a dependant, it cannot outlive the family's members and, when there is no longer a family to fulfil the contract, residential staff will be left to care alone.

The consequences that such changes in the life cycle, circumstances, and composition of a family have for residential workers, are similar to those which are part of the situation of staff in alternative communities. They are left with the dilemma of whether to step in and take on the caretaking role or whether to work at developing links with other resources which will provide an alternative.

Residential workers who have sought to retain the time-limited, focused emphasis of their units appear to have adopted two main kinds of approach to tackling this problem of transition.

Some, as Kelly describes, insist that residents who are admitted to the unit come with a guarantee of alternative accommodation when they have successfully completed the unit's programme. This is established at the assessment and referral stage of contact and so involves early consideration of alternatives to the existing family base (Jansen 1980 : 150). In those units concerned to develop care-sharing a variation of this approach is the agreement of a contract on admission which spells out the limits of the unit's care commitment. Whether the unit is to be used for holiday periods, day care or night care, the contract is a means of clarifying the ongoing commitment from the community-based care resource, whether that is a resident's family or an alternative. It is also a means by which any change in commitment can be reviewed, so that residential staff can consider at an early stage the consequences of new demands for them.

This approach is one which adds to a unit's entry criteria and so may exclude individuals and families who are unable to bring with them a guarantee of the required alternatives. In essence, this approach balances issues of 'turnover' and 'exclusion'. Those pursuing it argue that it provides a means of managing transition in a planned way and guaranteeing resident turnover. In the long term this ensures a focused service which benefits a large number of residents and families. It also openly acknowledges the fact that it is not possible to use this kind of residential resource effectively without ensuring resettlement and transitional opportunities at the earliest possible stage.

A second approach to the problems of transition which has emerged over the last ten years or so has been to develop alternative resettlement opportunities linked exclusively to the unit. This follows the pattern adopted by some family-alternative units in as far as the unit aims to support non-familial groups of ex-residents. But for family-support units this pattern has been adopted as a way of providing an alternative when the family can no longer make a contribution, rather than as a preferred option to family care.

One interesting account of the development of such a scheme for mentally handicapped adults has been provided by D. and D. Race (1979). This scheme was devised in response to the concern expressed by some elderly parents that, when they were no longer able to provide care for their offspring, there would be no possibility of them being able to continue living in small households in the community. The programme evolved was designed to be used when family care was beginning to be difficult for parents to maintain. It provided a short period in a hostel during which small groups of residents were encouraged to get to know one another and were helped, where necessary, to learn basic skills of day to day living. From this experience, residents were moved on to live together in an unstaffed 'group home' where ongoing advice and support was provided by hostel as well as social work staff. After a period another link was added to this chain – ordinary housing for individual residents or groups of two or three who had spent some time in the group home.

Where both these approaches to the problems of transition have been developed, residential workers have found themselves involved in arguing for a share in resources which are required by other groups living in the community. In doing so they have found themselves having to counter the view that individuals who are in residential care have less need of such resources than those 'at risk' in the community. Faced with this response, it can be particularly difficult to sustain the argument that entry to a residential resource should be tied to the availability of an additional resettlement resource. It sounds greedy, yet since family care can never be guaranteed, it is a necessary demand if family-support units are to sustain their rehabilitative focus.

Silting

The failure to maintain a flexible, focused regime through which individual change and transition is achieved has been described by Apte, among others, as one of the key characteristics of rehabilitative residential communities (Apte 1968). 'Silting' is the label often used by practitioners to describe the way in which their units gradually lose their innovative, time-limited, approach and drift into a more traditional medium- or long-term response to providing care.

The discussions about the problems of referral to, and transition from, family-support units has already suggested why 'silting' is likely to emerge in this type of care. Both the acceptance of residents whose circumstances suggest that short-term residential intervention is unlikely to be helpful, and the retention of residents because of a lack of alternative living situations, will contribute significantly to 'silting' in any particular unit. Yet there is also another important factor at work – the attitudes and practice of the unit's staff.

At the heart of successful family-supplement care lies the ability of residential workers to use their skills to tackle individual and family problems in a way which relates the expectations of the unit to those likely to be encountered in the world outside. This makes enormous demands on the regimes and programmes which units develop. The expectation is of structured, focused work which breaks down the barriers between the residential experience and other life experiences, by continuously relating the lessons learned and solutions reached in the unit to situations with which residents and families are likely to be faced outside. There are many examples of how this is done in practice, by workers and individuals, or groups. But what is commonly encountered in this work is a tension which arises from attempting to use residential regimes as a means of working towards increased self-reliance in individuals or families.

In Race and Race's account of the group home scheme for mentally handicapped adults in Slough this is a theme which emerges in the description of the relationship between the hostel and the group home. The authors suggest that a clash emerged at times between the 'basic routine discipline considered necessary in the hostel' in which staff by the 'very nature of their job' got used to making decisions about the lives of those in their care, and the environment of the group home where residents worked out their own lives together without constant staff supervision. They comment that, although the group home was linked to the hostel, its existence appeared to threaten not only the purpose of the hostel but also its basic ground rules (Race and Race 1979).

It is likely that family-supplement units (whether they are working towards resettlement in the family or an alternative) will be continuously confronted with the problem of how to promote resident independence through a residential situation which can engender dependency. Family-supplement units need to be a means to an end, not an end in themselves, and achieving and sustaining this goal is difficult. Nobody finds it easy to work at making themselves redundant, and residential workers are not exceptions; yet in a number of senses this is what they need to aim to do for each resident with whom they work. If they do not, then the regimes and practices they develop may handicap rather than rehabilitate and so slow down the turnover of the unit. When this happens it often leads to staff raising questions about unsuitable family and resettlement situations, reflecting their own reluctance to accept alternatives to the care which they provide.

This is not a problem unique to workers in family-support units; any unit with a rehabilitative focus faces staff with this predicament. But what is unique to the workers in this area of care, is that a reluctance to let residents go may directly undermine the contribution they are making to supporting family care. To counteract the contribution to 'silting' which their own practice might make and so maintain the momentum of their work, residential workers need to see their task as encompassing both unit life and family life. If either is to predominate, it should be the needs of the family rather than the needs of the unit's regime.

The potential of family-supplement care

Residential workers who are attempting to use residential units to support and supplement family care are breaking new ground and challenging some of the core beliefs held about the relationship of residential care to family care. These beliefs inform a number of the policies and procedures of the organization in which workers in those kinds of units work and it is because of this that a number of common problems arise. The ways in which residential workers respond to such problems as referral, engaging families, transition, and silting are crucial to realizing the full potential of family-supplement forms of residential care; for some kinds of response appear to result all too quickly in the loss of a family-support function and the provision of a more traditional long-term substitute or alternative to family care.

As yet there are few accounts of the kind of strategies which workers in this type of unit have evolved for successfully tackling these problems, or discussions of the kind of skills required for developing and maintaining residential resources which play a 'back-up' or 'bolstering' role rather than a caretaking one. Yet experience suggests that there are very specific skills in relation to both work with clients and work with related welfare organizations which are crucial to exploiting the potential of this kind of unit.

Let us look at the question of skills first. The currently promoted view of family-supplement care is that residential workers should operate as social workers from, and through, a centre providing a range of care options. From this centre they should be seeking to provide support to families and individuals in crisis, rather than attempting to replace their care. The practice skills this approach calls on will be those which contribute to assessment, individual counselling, family therapy, day care, time-limited residential care, and resettlement; in other words, skills and techniques which span a wider range than the usual repertoire of the field social worker. To build and develop such a range of practice skills, in one centre, will depend on establishing a team of individuals whose joint work will encompass them. Without this foundation it is difficult to see how the potential of this form of care can be realized.

Payne's account of the establishment of a multipurpose centre for children provides an interesting example of one attempt to build such a team (Payne and White 1979 : 125). The centre in question offered not only residential assessment and time-limited residential care but also facilities for pre-school and remedial education. The structure developed was a federal one in which areas of specialism, calling on specific worker skills, could be developed with maximum autonomy. In addition, in order to provide some coherence and consistency to the work being undertaken with residents' families, a specialist social work post was created with responsibilities for communicating and working with the home base and other agencies involved with the family.

In units which are innovating in this way there are few existing models of teamwork on which to draw. As the recent studies of social services teams have shown (Parsloe and Stevenson 1979) the dominant mode of teamwork in field social work is one in which a group of workers operates on the basis of individual caseloads, with virtually no sharing of tasks and skills through co-operative work. This way of organizing intervention has little to offer residential workers who necessarily use their knowledge and skills through working with colleagues and who cannot separate out their 'workload' in such an individualized way.

The discussion of problem areas has suggested that the effective implementation of family-supplement care is heavily dependent on the establishment of policy and management which is supportive of this kind of innovation. A residential resource concerned to bolster family care and to share caring responsibility has to be viewed as an integral part of a range of welfare provision for particular client groups. To return to Payne's account,

> 'the tasks of "rehabilitation" are perhaps the most difficult, and the process the least understood, in the whole helping effort. Our experience underscored the need to pay much closer attention to the "linkages" between the residential environment, the family of origin, and future foster or group care setting and, of equal importance, to the functions of residential and field social workers in achieving placement objectives. Care and "situational' treatment are not good enough by themselves and residential centres will fail in their purpose as long as they function in isolation.'
>
> (Payne and White 1979 : 149)

Residential staff cannot achieve these 'linkages' alone. The task they are attempting to fulfil needs to be explicitly recognized in the policies and management practice of their employing organizations. They need support and resources in exploring what is a new approach to residential care. It may well be the case that family-supplement care cannot reach its full potential within the current organization of statutory and voluntary social services in Britain. After all, this organization has evolved from a view of residential units as a means of containing problems rather than intervening in them. As a result, the professional and administrative traditions and boundaries which have developed may not be sensitive to the aims and objectives of family-supplement care.

One's view of how, and whether, the practice of family-supplement care is likely to spread, depends on one's view of the position of residential care in Britain today. The view of the 'optimists', described in chapter one, suggests that the changes needed to realize the potential of this type of care will occur when there are enough trained workers in the area sharing a common base of knowledge and skills to develop innovative approaches in residential practice and management. However, the 'pessimists' and 'radicals' would suggest that attempts to develop family-supplement care will have to grapple with a more fundamental problem than professional training. The dominant ideas about the relationship between the family and welfare provision in Britain are in conflict with the assumptions which underlie family-supplement care. For the pessimists, the potential of this form of care is bound to be constrained by a broader welfare ideology.

Summary

The notion of using residential care as a means of supplementing and supporting family care has been promoted relatively recently and there are still very few written accounts of the experiences of residential workers who have tried to realize it.

Looking across the current range of units offering this kind of care, it is possible to distinguish three main types. There are those which work to rehabilitate families; those which focus on rehabilitating the individual to family life; and those which share the care of dependants with families. In each of these types of unit the problems being faced by workers have centred on their difficulties in establishing and maintaining the time-limited purposive nature of their work.

The problems which surround referral are central here. For the idea of supporting family care suggests that a residential resource should be used at an early stage, when there is still a chance of the family working with their difficulties. The early involvement of residential workers in this way calls into question the typical division of responsibility and function between field and residential social workers.

The kind of planned and focused intervention which is vital to the success of family-supplement care means that the problems workers face in engaging the family are substantially different from those which typify family-substitute and family-alternative care. It is not just that the family may become clients, but that they may also become co-workers and co-managers in a care-sharing unit.

Family-supplement care aims for the return of residents to their families and the community, but it cannot guarantee this outcome. Staff need to grapple with the problem of providing alternative residential resources, as well as considering the effects of using their own unit as an alternative living situation for some residents.

A final, and recurring, problem faced by workers in this kind of unit is that of 'silting'; the loss of impetus and direction in a unit's programme, resulting in a change in its use. The suggestion is that there are several contributory factors to this process, which workers need to grasp. They include the ways in which workers' own styles help or hinder the development of independence in residents.

In considering the potential of family-supplement care, one becomes aware of the challenge it presents to existing professional, organizational, and administrative structures. Its development is, therefore, dependent on a number of fundamental shifts in attitudes, as well as the encouragement and support of this kind of innovation by management in the statutory and voluntary services.

6

The residential task

Residential care has now been considered historically and in terms of the main function which residential units are currently adopting in relation to family care. In pursuing these themes, the emphasis so far has been on the range of different expectations being made of residential workers.

In this chapter the discussion of the task of residential workers is extended by focusing on some of the common expectations they face. This focus reflects the concern which has emerged over the last fifteen years in the social work literature to identify the core elements of the residential task. Those elements underlie the contribution of all workers, regardless of the client group they work with or the type of unit they work in.

Not surprisingly, in considering these core elements, it is impossible to ignore the relationship between residential care and the family. Attempts to identify and describe the task and associated skills of the residential worker have moved through two stages. The first has sought to establish that a distinction exists between the task of those working in residential units and the task of those caring in the family. The second has attempted to show that the tasks and skills of residential workers can be viewed as part of the activity of social work.

The residential task and family care

The emergence of the first stage can be traced to the attempt in the immediate post-war period to break with the Poor Law traditions of state residential care. This attempt, as chapter two showed, drew heavily on the alternative analogy of family life and, in doing so, tended to use attributes found in 'good' mothers (and occasionally fathers) as a baseline against which to measure the suitability of residential workers. One consequence of this was that it reinforced the view that residential work was nothing more or less than family life on a larger scale. The task of those employed in it and the skills they needed to acquire became closely equated with such 'natural' characteristics as 'practical common sense', 'warmth', and 'household management'.

The first sustained attempt to question this way of thinking can be found in the Williams Committee Report. This report, which examined the state of residential care in the early 1960s, challenged the 'commonly held misconception' that the task undertaken by residential workers was identical 'to that of any housewife with a fairly large family'. In the Committee's view residential work needed to be regarded quite differently. It needed to be seen as an occupation which required specialist knowledge and skills and therefore specialist training. As an occupation its prime task was determined by the one demand which all residents made:

'They all need understanding and help for themselves as individuals. It is the sustaining of personality with which the worker is concerned and his task, though it will vary in method, is basically the same in purpose and intention for all ages and all groups.'

(Williams 1967)

The method described as essential to the realization of this task, was the creation of friendly, happy residential communities which were responsive to their members' needs for dependence and independence. The report did not spell out in detail the skills which would contribute to the creation of such communities, but it did suggest, in broad terms, the kind of knowledge base such a task required. This base, which included a knowledge of human growth and development, group behaviour and social administration, had much in common with that transmitted in social work training. In addition, the committee argued for recognition of the fact that those who had responsibility for managing units also required knowledge which would enable them to develop the specific 'technical skills' required for unit management and staff support.

The Committee suggested, then, that it was possible to identify a task which was common to all forms of residential work and was clearly distinct from the task of a housewife or mother. Having identified that task, the Committee felt it important to draw a distinction between the two kinds of residential workers who contributed to it – care staff and heads of home; for each carried particular responsibilities to which a specific range of skills was relevant.

Following the work of the Williams Committee, the discussion of the residential task was developed further in relation to one particular area of residential care – work with children. The Castle Priory Report is particularly significant here, in that it not only argued that it was time to move away from the image of residential workers as substitute parents, but that it was also important to move away from the type of unit which reflected this image:

> 'Family group homes tend to copy family life instead of recognising the value of small groups within the structure of somewhat larger establishments. They over-emphasize the traditional family concept without, in fact, providing the security which a real family gives. Staff are often isolated and unsupported within them and too many roles have to be played by them.'   (Kahan and Banner 1972)

The alternative model the report offered was one in which residential workers would practise as professionals who provided residential 'treatment' in units which were run as therapeutic communities. This was an alternative firmly based on the notion that the residential task centred on the provision of warm, supportive, and enabling relationships. Although the report did not specify what it meant by a therapeutic community, it did specify, in some detail, what it considered to be the major elements of the worker's task, as well as the knowledge and skill base on which professional training for the task should be established.

The report argued that the residential worker's task in the child care field has two major elements: 'nurturing care' and 'remedial care'. The first of these comprised those functions normally undertaken by parents – functions which foster the emotional and physical development of a child, by offering opportunities through which he can develop his abilities, understand himself and others, master his feelings, and develop a sense of personal identity. Nurturing care was care which sought to meet the basic needs of all children. In contrast the second element of the task – the provision of 'remedial care' – was particular to the needs of children living in residential units. Such children, the report suggested, come from a 'highly selective population group' who had experienced difficulties in their home life as well as difficulties in separating from their natural parents. Whilst the way in which these difficulties were experienced were unique to each child the report maintained that it was possible to identify special needs likely to arise in all children living in residential care. These were generated by problems resulting from separation and were seen as 'likely to involve feelings of rejection, shock, which is manifested physically as well as emotionally, emotional blocking combined with phantasy, resentment, increased dependency and depression'.

It was through 'remedial care', the report suggested, that the residential workers recognized and met these needs. They did so by helping children with their immediate feelings and behaviour problems and by recognizing that, because of poor ego development, wishes to regress and problems over impulse control were highly likely to arise.

In their description of the skills which workers need to undertake this task the report emphasized skills in working with individuals, working with and through groups, and structuring daily routines. They identified these skills as part of the repertoire of fieldwork social workers and concluded that they could be imparted through a common social work training. Yet in discussing the conditions in which these skills could be realistically implemented, the report stated that an increase in staff-resident ratios and a clearer distinction between caring and housekeeping functions were essential.

What is particularly interesting about the way in which this report tackles the relationship between family care and the residential task is that, in outlining an alternative to a family model of residential care, it still draws heavily on notions of what family life gives to children. Thus, 'nurturing care' (as Beedell's detailed account suggests) rests heavily on ideas about what parents 'normally' provide for their children. The suggestion is that the fundamental distinction between a residential worker providing 'parenting' and a parent providing it, lies not so much in content as in the purpose to which the activity is put.

Important, too, is the argument which this report develops in considering the allocation of domestic work in residential units. The theme running through the report is that residential workers need to be freed from some of the routine working, cleaning, and mending in order to be able to provide residential treatment and fully realize the task set them. But, it is suggested, they cannot abandon all domestic responsibilities; some domestic labour is essential to the provision of both nurturing and remedial care and, therefore, a distinction needs to be made between this and the 'housekeeping functions' which distract workers from their professional tasks.

In attempting to separate the element of domestic work inherent in the residential task from the kind of domestic labour which hinders it, the report highlights a crucial area of difficulty for those attempting to clarify the task of the residential worker. If one looks at domestic labour in family households for a comparison, it is clear that, typically, most of it is the responsibility of adult women who combine it with the care of dependants. In suggesting that there should be a clearer distinction between 'housekeeping functions' and 'caring work' in residential units for children, the report both breaks with, and reinforces, the comparison between residential care and family life. It breaks with it in suggesting that the provision of 'adequate caring' is dependent on adult careers being freed from some of the daily grind of domestic work – not a situation which is common to most families – but it reinforces it in the sense that, in suggesting this work should be allocated to a separate group of domestic workers, it promotes a distribution of domestic labour within units by which women carry the larger part.

The residential task and social work

The concern of the Castle Priory Report to 'professionalize' the residential task both by freeing it from its 'family' image and by freeing residential workers from basic domestic labour, heralds the second stage in identifying the task – that of attempting to align it with social work. This theme reflects the changes in the organization of both the residential services and social work training which took place in Britain in the early 1970s.

As part of these changes, in 1973 the Central Council for Education and Training in Social Work (CCETSW) turned its attention to the nature of the residential worker's task. In its report the Council suggested that residential work was best seen as 'a method of social work on an equal footing with casework, community work and groupwork – part with them of the common helping process of social work. As a method of social work, residential work shared, they argued, a common core of goals, values, knowledge, clients, and skills with the other methods. Its uniqueness stemmed from the particular organizational context in which its practitioners operated – the residential centre.

The report identified six activities common to all residential centres.

(1) Social work – which included work providing individual care programmes, supporting families, mobilizing community and centre resources, and working with groups.
(2) Personal services – which included the provision of food, clothing, help in daily living, and recreational facilities.
(3) Personnel management – which included developing staff skills.
(4) Administration of and forward planning for the centre.
(5) Providing facilities for student training.
(6) Other functions – which included, public relations, operational planning, and interprofessional cooperation.

These were activities to which the whole range of staff employed in residential centres were seen as contributing in varying degrees. While a distinction was made between 'social work' tasks and 'personal service' tasks, it was recognized that in residential establishments it was often impossible to separate completely these two areas, or allocate them to particular members of staff.

In reaching this view of residential work and its associated tasks, the CCETSW working party had not begun with the kind of family comparisons which had been a relevant starting point for the Williams Committee, the Castle Priory Report, and other literature of the 1960s. The focus had shifted and it was the comparison between residential work and social work which now provided the basis from which to identify the nature of the residential task. In working through this comparison, the working party rejected the notion that the differences between the concerns and practice of residential work and social work outweighed the similarities. In particular, it rejected the view that the more varied and personal range of contact between residential worker and client required a more eclectic and broadly based knowledge and skill base than social work. In its opinion, residential work could be understood as sharing the core elements of social work, whilst developing in addition a specialist body of knowledge and skills.

In identifying those tasks and skills which it considered to be common to workers in all residential units, the working party put forward, but finally rejected, the idea that it was possible to distinguish between the basic and specialist care provided by a unit. In doing so, it promoted the notion that these were inseparable elements of the residential task. While this report resolved the question of an appropriate pattern of training (interestingly enough, one which incorporates two distinct types of qualification), it has by no means resolved the debate about the residential task. Other approaches have emerged since.

In 1976 a joint working party set up by the Residential Care Association (RCA) and the British Association of Social Workers (BASW) reported on the respective and reciprocal roles of residential workers and field social workers (RCA 1976). This looked at the traditional division of labour between residential and field social workers and commented that it appeared to result in the field social worker being most likely 'to be the person with responsibility for the major decisions affecting a client's life', while the residential worker was left 'with responsibility for the more mundane, less demanding and less satisfying tasks'.

The working party claimed that as a result residential workers had unsatisfactory and limited involvement in clients' problems. They were not involved early enough prior to admission; they played little part in decisions about discharge or work with a client's family; they were expected to end their relationship with the client on discharge. As far as the clients were concerned, there was a danger that this set division of professional responsibility and function resulted in a neglect of their needs, wishes, and interests.

The alternative the working party outlined was one which suggested a considerable extension of the responsibilities, and therefore the task, of residential workers. The idea promoted was that each client should have a 'key worker', a 'person having full accountability for the client received into residential care and for decisions relating to the case' (RCA 1976 : 347). This person could be a field or residential worker, and would be responsible for planning and implementing an individual care plan for the client.

The suggestion here was that the task of the residential worker should not solely be considered in terms of the demands made within a residential unit. Consideration also had to be given to those processes outside the unit which play a part in shaping a client's life. If this idea was to be pursued then the task residential workers would be called on to fulfil would include whole areas which have traditionally been the domain of field social workers. In covering these areas, residential workers would need to develop appropriate assessment, planning, and care management skills.

However, this extension of the boundaries of the residential task would not be solely dependent on residential workers' interest in, and ability to develop, the appropriate skills. The kind of role-blurring the key worker concept suggests raises a number of questions about the current organization of field and residential work within the statutory and voluntary services. The few written accounts of attempts to implement it have suggested that it does not fit easily with existing administrative structures (Bromley 1977; Allen 1977).

A year later a BASW working party report, *The Social Work Task*, took the view that only some of the tasks undertaken by residential workers could be regarded as social work tasks as such. 'Social work in a residential setting consists of various activities which will be common to many other caring situations, together with aspects which are more specific to social work' (BASW 1977). The characteristics which distinguish the distinctly social work elements of the residential task are described as including: the purposeful use of group interaction to enhance the personal and social functioning of an individual and the upholding of a professional code of ethics.

In contrast, a recent RCA document has approached the question by outlining what it considers to be those elements of social work practice common to all settings and has then distinguished those elements which appear unique to residential settings. They suggest that the unique elements include: 'total care; prolonged client contact; intensity of relationships; extensive use of groupwork techniques; the danger of expectations on the part of the clients of excessive dependency' (RCA 1977 : 13). Their conclusion is that all these have specific implications for the development and application of social work skills, which need to be worked through by residential practitioners.

These attempts to be definitive about similarity and difference between social work and residential work have been generated by the concern to establish the professional credibility of the residential work task by bringing it into the mainstream of social work. As a result, a lot of energy has been spent focusing on those elements in residential care which 'fit' existing definitions of social work, yet agreement on the basis of this 'fit' has been difficult to reach. While some argue that all residential work can be viewed as a method of social work, others see only some elements of residential work reflecting the social work task, and others argue for the reorganization of the boundaries between both. Whatever position has been taken, the result has been that the distinct unity of the residential worker's task has tended to slip from view. This is because the stress has been on trying to fragment the task into 'social work' and 'non-social work' elements. The problem is that these distinctions tend to hold at only a very general level of discussion and any detailed examination of the activities residential workers are engaged in, shows how little consideration has been given to the unique and complex problems of client–worker interaction resulting from the demands made on residential units. If these problems were identified as being of central concern to social workers, then it is likely that some helpful additions would be made to the existing literature. For example, the issue of control in residential work has a number of unique dimensions which tend to be lost when consideration of the residential task fragments it into social work and non-social work elements. Yet these dimensions are of crucial importance when attempting to innovate and develop staff practice in residential units (Dharamsi *et al.* 1979 : 264).

When one looks at current attempts to analyse the residential task it becomes apparent that most contributors to the debate have leaned heavily on the notion of client need as a means of steering their passage through the similarities and differences between family care on the one hand and social work on the other. It is a notion which has been used as a means of establishing both the focus and the boundary of the task. For some it has been the starting point for a consideration of the residential task:

'The focus of the Working Party's concern is the individual. We believe that caring for people in residential centres involves concern for the total needs of individuals; these include spiritual, emotional, physical and educational needs.'

(CCETSW 1973 : 8)

For others, it has been seen as a core element in the residential task:

> 'The essential task, as we see it, is to devise a system of residential care which gives proper weight to the special handicaps and needs of people, but which does not, by offering them care, alienate them from the rest of the community. It must be a system which acknowledges the needs, interests and hopes which are common to us all.'   (PSSC 1975 : 14)

For yet others it has been used as the means of distinguishing the elements which should be common to residential and field social work:

> 'Our belief is that either the field social worker or the residential social worker could take the responsibility for making professional decisions regarding a client, within or entering residential care, and that the worker undertaking this responsibility should be nominated because of his, or her, appropriateness to meet the client's needs rather than because of the post held.'   (RCA 1976)

In other words, client need has emerged as a pivotal concept in clarifying ideas about the form and content of the residential task. Because of the importance which has been placed on it in discussions of the task, the next section of this chapter critically considers some of the typical examples of its use.

Client need

A concern with the individual client, his life situation, and his needs has always been central to the activity of social work. Those writers in the field of residential care who argue that the starting point for any systematic consideration of the residential task must be the relationship between client need and residential practice, are, therefore, following a well-established social work tradition. There are numerous examples of this approach, but a brief outline of two will serve to highlight the essential assumptions that it makes.

Beedell, in his discussion of residential provision for children, places considerable emphasis on identifying the needs of this client group. He argues that the central purpose of residential provision for children is to enable them to develop as individuals who will be able to return eventually to their families, foster families, or an independent life in the community. From this position he attempts to outline client need in some detail, as well as the kind of residential provision which should ensure that these needs are met (Beedell 1970).

He suggests that healthy individual development in children is essentially dependent on three kinds of provision: protection from danger, discomfort and distress; opportunities for intellectual, social and physical growth; and the growth and maintenance of personal integrity. This provision is usually made in natural family groupings by 'parenting' – 'the arrangements which any society makes for its children to be reared, learn the accepted cultural patterns and reach toward expected standards of adult individuality and responsibility' (Beedell 1970 : 17). For Beedell, when responsibility for 'parenting' is taken over by a residential unit, workers in that unit must consciously attempt to provide 'parenting' which is at least as good as that provided by an ordinary family and 'in some respects more expertly related to the child's individual needs'. Residential workers should therefore provide care, comfort and control; nurturing; and opportunities for the development and maintenance of personal integrity.

It is from a discussion of these three kinds of provision for need that Beedell develops his view of the distinctive elements of residential care for children; a view which ties 'client need' closely to a notion of what is recognized and provided for in 'ordinary' family life.

Another example of discussions of the residential task which is firmly based on client need is Brearley's book *Residential Work with the Elderly* (Brearley 1977). Brearley argues that to understand and develop practice in this field residential workers should have a firm grasp of the general needs of older people as a group, as well as the specific needs which individuals bring to residential units. For Brearley the general needs of this client group are rooted in the particular social and psychological stage they have reached in their life cycle. His suggestion is that satisfaction in old age depends on the balance which the individual achieves between 'inner needs' and 'external pressures'. Broadly, these 'inner needs' relate to emotional growth and adjustment, while 'external pressures' relate to financial, material, and physical circumstances.

In Brearley's view, individuals who are admitted to residential units have necessarily reached a crisis in relation to this 'balance' and the circumstances of this crisis, together with entry to residential care, will generate specific individual needs which residential workers should recognize and respond to.

The relationship between client need and the residential task suggested here, is one which rests on a distinction between needs which are general to a client group and those which are specific to any individual client. General needs are shaped by the social circumstances and development stage of a particular client group, and the principal task of any residential unit in relation to these needs should be to provide opportunities in which further growth and development are at least possibilities. In contrast, specific needs are shaped by the particular circumstances which have resulted in an individual's admission to residential care and the impact of entry to residential care on them. The principal task of the residential unit in relation to these needs should be to provide an environment in which the individual can recover from the crisis of admission and the problems which preceded it.

Whilst Brearley focuses on the elderly as a client group, he does generalize from his analysis: 'The fundamental problem of any individual, at any age, admitted to an institution, is the conflict between the need to feel safe, secure and wanted and the need to remain an independent, integrated whole person' (Brearley 1977 : 67). He argues that the essence of residential work is to maintain 'a balance between these two needs', suggesting a further dimension to the relationship between client need and the residential task, which is of relevance to all client groups.

Brearley's approach does not tie the definition of client need to a particular view of family life, it suggests instead that it is helpful to define need on the basis of an understanding of human growth and development. It also suggests that it is possible to view admission to residential care both as the result of specific problems which an individual faces in meeting his needs and as an event which itself generates specific needs in each individual.

While these are just two examples of attempts to clarify the scope of the residential task by drawing on the concept of client need, they do raise some basic questions about this particular approach to the question.

First, the term 'client need' is used to make a number of generalized claims about the characteristics of particular groups who find themselves in residential care. When these claims are examined, it is clear that they should be viewed with some caution, given the evidence on which they appear to be based. Beedell's discussion of the needs of children, for example, is dependent on a particular view of what constitutes 'parenting' in an 'ordinary' family; a view which identifies a number of the core characteristics of this activity and therefore stresses similarity rather than difference between nuclear families in British society. Yet there are a number of studies, for example those by the Newsons (1968; 1976), which demonstrate the existence of differences in both the opportunities provided by ordinary families and the style of 'parenting' they adopt.

Similarly, Brearley's statements about the 'general' needs of particular client groups stress similarity rather than differences within such groups. It is a view based on a particular notion of human growth and development; a notion which needs to be critically examined by workers before it is accepted as a foundation for analysing the residential task.

Brearley's discussion of the specific needs of individuals admitted to care pinpoints the importance of recognizing that the circumstances surrounding admission and the impact of admission should have a key influence on the relationships which develop between workers and residents. However, the work of Goffmann, Balberni, Hoghughi and others, suggests that there are problems in attempting to understand this complex social process solely in terms of individual client need and worker response.

In his discussion of residential care for adolescents, Tutt (1978) suggests that those who view admission to care as a reflection of specific client needs, accept a perspective which focuses solely on the inadequacies of the individual entering care and the 'treatment' needed to 'cure' those inadequacies. It is a perspective which can blind workers to the recognition that factors resulting in admission to residential care can be located in very different sources; for example, the needs of a key caretaker, the lack of alternative welfare provision, or the break-up of the family.

My suggestion is that the term 'client need' has been used in discussions of the residential task in a way which conveys a number of implicit assumptions about family life, the characteristics of the client group, and the causes and impact of admission to care. When workers read or use the term they need to be sensitive to the purpose which it is serving. At present it is used to mean many things in different contexts.

The second major point which should be made about this term is that a number of writers using it have conveyed the idea that the activities of a residential unit and its workers are, or should ideally be, influenced by client need above all else. In practice, of course, residential units are complex organizations whose activities cannot be understood by reducing them to an equation in which client need is matched by worker response.

Tizard and his colleagues in studying residential units for children, suggested that there were four key, interrelated variables which appeared to shape the task undertaken in residential establishments (Tizard, Sinclair, and Clarke 1975 : 5):

(1) The ideology of the unit – its philosophy and approach.
(2) The structure of the unit – its size, autonomy, and staffing structure.
(3) The attitudes of unit staff.
(4) The response of residents.

In other words, client need is most realistically seen as just one of a number of variables which shape the residential task. As such it is most usefully viewed in the total context of a particular residential unit. Its relationship to other key variables should be considered because it is a product of particular residential situations, as well as an influence on them.

Towards a definition of the residential task

Faced with so little general agreement about the nature and boundaries of their task, residential workers, when called on to describe their work, usually find themselves left to the resources of their own experience. The problems this can generate have already been described in chapters three, four and five. It is impossible for staff to establish and realize aims, to initiate and sustain innovation, and to change their practice, unless they have some idea of their task that stretches beyond the immediacy of the daily demands to which they are responding.

There are, as yet, few detailed written accounts of the experiences of workers who have tried to clarify their task in the course of their daily practice. The Harlesden project, mentioned earlier in this book, is an exception (Dharamsi *et al.* 1979): The team of workers employed in this project attempted, from the outset, to work together in clarifying and agreeing aims for their unit and tasks for their team. They provide a vivid account of the difficulties they faced in doing this and, in concluding their discussion of the process involved, comment:

> 'At the end of two years' residential social work we had mixed feelings about our aims for care and about the care we had provided. It was generally felt from outside the project that we had held and operated a coherent "philosophy" of care and that we had achieved some definition of residential tasks. Workers on the other hand, knew they had had a number of unresolved internal differences about aims and tasks.'   (Dharamsi *et al.* 1979 : 262)

In drawing out the implications of this experience for workers in similar projects, they make two main points. First, that employing organizations, such as social service departments, need to engage in deeper discussion aimed at clarifying for themselves the aims and tasks of residential child care. Second, that residential workers need to be provided with increased opportunities and external support to work on the aims and task of their individual units.

The Harlesden workers felt sure, however, that there are limits to achieving agreement in this area, because discussions of aims and tasks in residential work with children, at whatever level they take place, are bound to expose the existing 'confusions, ambiguities and even conflicts, in general notions of child care' (Dharamsi *et al.* 1979 : 263).

There are a number of important points here which need to be born in mind, when considering the direction workers might take in clarifying their idea of task and attempting to realize it in their practice. First it is clear that there is a need for both the unit staff and the managers of the employing organization to work on this issue. Second, it is likely that there will be ongoing differences of perspective. Third, it is inevitable that there will be problems of realizing statements of aims and task in the daily encounters between residents, workers, management, and the wider community. Yet, despite these difficulties, the pursuit of this issue within a unit appears to provide staff with a sense of purpose and insight into the problems which confront them.

Residential workers who are interested in pursuing this issue in practice may find it useful to adapt one of the following two approaches as guidelines. The first has been constructed by L. Ward (Walton and Elliott 1980 : 25), the second is the framework developed by the Personal Social Services Council (PSSC 1977).

Ward provides a detailed statement of the five main areas of work which she considers to be central to the residential social work task. Her concern is to suggest how workers can undertake these activities in a way which proves beneficial to those entering residential care. She suggests that residential staff should clarify and agree their task by starting from the premise that residential admission represents a breakdown that has occurred at two interacting levels. First, 'the *personal* experience of breakdown for the individual concerned, the meaning of admission for *him* in terms of his own functioning, behaviour, relationships and life-situation'; and, second, 'breakdown at the interpersonal level, the breakdown *between* the individual and his family, *between* him and important others, *between* him and his social environment, school or work, peer group, neighbourhood and community' (Walton and Elliott 1980 : 25).

Such breakdowns, Ward argues, generate particular resident needs, and in responding fully to these needs, residential workers intervene at two interacting levels; with 'the person and his personal states and processes' and with 'the person and his outside world'. It is these responses which shape the two main aspects of the worker's task, which are: '(I) working with individuals in the context of the group inside *the residential unit* and (II) with the residents individually and through the group, across *the unit's boundaries*' (Walton and Elliott 1980 : 25).

Both these aspects of the task must, in Ward's view, balance the meeting of individual resident need with ensuring that there is an acceptable role for the unit within society. This balance can be achieved by workers, and their management bodies, defining and agreeing residential care objectives. Such objectives should include the operational purpose of the unit, what it hopes to achieve, who it is intended should benefit from it, and how it aims to function. 'When objectives are shared, understood and accepted both within the residential centre and across its boundaries, agreement can be reached between the team of workers and the (higher order) management body regarding policy and practice' (Walton and Elliott 1980 : 27).

For the workers in any unit it is the detailed definition of these objectives which clarify the unit's basic functions, and hence the framework within which they fulfil their task. While such objectives will differ between units, there are also some objectives which Ward suggests are basic to all units. For example, 'a basic objective of any caring establishment is to assess and respond to the needs of the client group'. In achieving this in a positive fashion, workers must question the assumption that they have a greater understanding of residents' needs than the residents themselves. Ward points out that if residents do not have the opportunities to fulfil their own needs, then the residential care experience is likely to be a depersonalizing one. To realize the residential task in this area, workers and residents must share responsibility for need fulfilment.

What Ward's approach offers workers is a means of linking the residential task (based on a particular notion of client need) with a process of clarifying and agreeing objectives, policy, and care practices in any one unit. She argues that this link is vital if workers are to create residential solutions which are of positive value to those using them.

The PSSC framework was developed as part of a study of adult residential care, which discovered a great deal of uncertainty and insecurity among residential staff about their task and practice. It is intended that it should be used by residential workers to consider systematically the needs of residents and develop the kind of care practices which will best meet those needs (PSSC 1977 : 9).

The PSSC document suggests that staff should work at clarifying and agreeing their care objectives in three main ways. First, in relation to residential care as a welfare service; second, in relation to the particular form of care each unit provides; third, in relation to each individual who receives or gives care.

As far as general principles are concerned, the PSSC document takes the view that these should be shaped by a consideration of the residents' experiences of care. It is their contention that residential care for adults should aim to maximize the opportunities for residents to 'live as normally as possible in a situation where their individuality, independence and personal dignity are respected.' To achieve this, the rights of residents to participate, take risks, use general community services, and make decisions, need to be recognized and protected. The difficulties which might be raised in implementing these rights are noted, but it is argued that:

'all those concerned with the well-being of people in homes should acknowledge the validity of these rights and try to promote them. Their implementation is bound to involve some risk for residents both individually and as a group. Staff will therefore need considerable support in order to resist any well-intentioned, but sometimes misguided, pressures or attack from families, the general public or the press.'   (PSSC 1977 : 10)

The document stresses the importance for every organization providing care of publishing a clear statement of principles in order to publicize policies, focus discussion, and challenge (or offer a check on) the distortion of policies.

These principles are seen as the foundation on which the specific obectives for individual units can be established. The PSSC document outlines in some detail how unit objectives are likely to vary according to client group, the nature of demand, the number of other residential units, and the availability of alternative services. It suggests that, with objectives defined and the purpose of the home established, the daily routine and care practices appropriate to a unit will evolve.

These routines and practices are seen as being influenced by the third set of objectives – the objectives for individual residents. For, depending on the objectives set for the care of an individual, it may prove necessary to modify those set for the home, as well as aspects of its daily routine. The PSSC argues that objectives should not only be defined for each resident, but that the best means of attaining them should be spelt out and recorded so that they are 'kept in view' by all concerned. It suggests in detail how this might be done and what implications this has for the residential work task (PSSC 1977 : 21).

Defining objectives in this way provides a means of reviewing and evaluating the work of a unit, the progress of the individual resident, and the performance of staff. It also provides residents, staff, families, and others with a focus for discussing difficulties which may arise between them.

It is interesting how this approach to defining task and developing appropriate practice stresses individual 'rights' as well as 'needs'. This stress echoes some of the recent concerns expressed by residents whose experience of care suggests that normally accepted individual rights can be neglected (Kahan 1979; Paige and Clarke 1977).

Summary

This chapter has attempted to explore the current debate about the nature of the residential task. In doing so it has traced a concern, in the literature, to distinguish that task from the care undertaken in the family and, more recently, to stress the similarities between the residential task and social work. The suggestion here has been that this approach has tended to fragment the task as residential workers experience it and has allowed unique areas of concern to slip from view. What is more, it has not established any real measure of agreement which workers can use in their everyday practice.

Contributors to the debate on the residential task have made a great deal of use of the notion of client need. In looking at two typical examples of the use of this notion, it is clear that it has been used to describe a wide range of individual characteristics and social processes and therefore should be regarded with some caution when it is encountered in discussions of residential care.

Finally, this chapter has considered the advantages to workers of deepening their understanding of the task in which they are engaged and has outlined two approaches which could be used to do so. Both emphasize the need to establish agreement about aims, objectives, and tasks, not only within the unit but between the unit and the employing agency. Both also emphasize the importance of basing discussions of task on recognition of the needs and rights of individual residents in any unit.

7

The future of residential care

In drawing together the threads of this discussion of residential solutions, it is impossible to ignore how often the terms 'potential' and 'possibility' have been used. This has not been an accident, it has reflected the difficulty of attempting to assess a service whose past and present performance give such little hope for optimism. As Righton states, 'if there is one social service more consistently stormed at by shot and shell than any other, it is residential care' (Righton 1976 : 10). From the left and right of the political spectrum, from social work academics and practitioners, the response to residential care has tended to be a highly critical one.

The climate of the last twenty years or so has been particularly critical. Social workers, amongst others, have persistently questioned the value of most residential solutions not only on the basis of their direct experience of them, but also on the basis of a growing body of evidence which suggests that typically they have destructive and depersonalizing effects. This evidence is not just a product of the various psychological and sociological studies of institutional life. An increasing number of residents' accounts of their own experiences (for example, N. Arden's *A Child of the System* (1977), J. Deacon's *Tongue Tied* (1974), E. Newton's *This Bed My Centre* (1980)) highlight the negative aspects of residential care. In doing so they contrast it with home and family life.

A focus on the potential of various forms of residential care is, in essence, an attempt to look beyond the current scene to a future in which residential solutions might actually benefit the majority of those using them. A future in which the belief now dominating theory and practice 'that life in a nuclear family, however bad, is superior to life in a residential community, however good' (Righton 1976 : 11), gives way to a realization that there may be alternative forms of communal living which are viable and satisfying.

Because controversy exists about the likelihood of such a future being realized, and because differences exist between those who talk about change in residential care, this last chapter looks at the future of the residential services.

Future scope

The emphasis of current discussion is on the need to reduce the scope of residential care by finding alternative solutions to the social, economic, and personal difficulties which result in thousands of individuals becoming 'residents'. The arguments used to support this view stem from both professional and financial concerns. They often fuse and it is difficult to disentangle them, but each needs to be considered on its own merits if the rationale for contraction is to be clearly understood.

Let us look at the professional concerns first. The stress which social workers place on the negative outcomes of residential care have generated two main arguments for contraction in the professional literature. The first suggests that a more limited use of residential solutions would make this form of intervention more purposive and positive in outcome. The second suggests that in order to realize a social work approach to residential care, particular kinds of care will need to be contracted.

Righton provides one example of the first argument in his examination of the positive and negative aspects of our current provision (Righton 1977). He sees a more beneficial service being provided if residential care is used in a time-limited way and restricted to five main groups. In his view, time-limited residential care is a means of ensuring a positive use of this form of intervention, while its restriction to individuals for whom other alternatives are not viable ensures that it no longer serves as a 'dustbin'. The groups he identifies as those who should benefit from this smaller, more specialized service are as follows.

(1) Children and adolescents who have been emotionally damaged in their own families.
(2) Children and adolescents who are a risk to themselves and others.
(3) Children and adolescents needing 'intensive but specific social experience of a kind families cannot easily provide'.
(4) People needing continuous attention or specific treatment or whose disability, frailty or behaviour puts intolerable strain on others, even when day care and domiciliary facilities are available.
(5) People of any age learning to cope with independent living after prolonged spells in hospital.

The notion here is of contraction producing a service which is far narrower in scope and shaped by much clearer objectives. Its implementation would mean that thousands of individuals currently living in residential units would be 'de-institutionalized' and those entering in future would do so for limited periods and for clearly specified reasons.

This position is one supported by the evidence from a number of studies which have suggested that many individuals in residential care could manage their lives successfully in alternative forms of accommodation. These studies have covered the range of groups in residential care – the elderly, the mentally and physically disabled, and children. Several surveys, of the residents of elderly persons' homes for example, have shown that significant numbers could manage in their own homes with the regular support of community services or in specially adapted or sheltered housing. Despite the fact that the percentage of elderly people in the population has been growing steadily and will continue to do so in the 1980s, commentators such as Townsend (1973) and Bosanquet (1978) argue that policies designed to expand special housing and support services could still result in a considerable reduction in the demand for places in residential units. Similar arguments have been developed in relation to mentally and physically disabled adults (Morris 1969). On the same lines, studies of children in residential care (Rowe and Lambert 1973) have suggested that, with an increase in fostering and intensive material and casework support given to some families, thousands of children could leave residential units. This indicates that there needs to be a link between contraction of residential care and the expansion of the use of other welfare services, such as income maintenance; housing; domiciliary services; intermediate treatment; field social work and warden-assisted accommodation. These are services which are intended not only to boost and sustain the efforts of families to care, but also to provide non-residential substitutes for family care.

Alongside this argument for the contraction of residential provision, is another option currently being promoted by some social work commentators as a blueprint for the future. It is the idea of contracting specific areas of residential care, and developing others, in an attempt to change the nature of residential solutions so that they become increasingly beneficial to their users. This option reflects the incrementally positive view of 'the optimists' discussed in chapter one, in that, while it accepts the evidence of the negative effects of residential care, it promotes the idea that such effects are reversible if residential units adopt a social work approach to caring.

Ward, for example, suggests that it is useful to view the functions which residential units perform as having three main outcomes: institutionalization; residential care; and residential intervention. The first of these occurs when a residential unit is used as a container for those who are found to pose problems for society – a 'dustbin' for the unwanted. The second occurs when a residential unit acts to promote 'group living' or 'optional life fulfilment within the context of an ongoing shared group experience, and a selectively planned environment'. The third occurs when a residential unit acts as

> 'a dynamic social work resource; purposefully selected to meet an individual's defined needs. It is a way of offering a child or an adult opportunity for evaluating personal and social situations within a supportive environment; for working with problems through exposure to interpersonal interaction with other members of the group and through supported interaction across the boundaries of the residential unit. It involves establishing goals, determining strategies and stabilising positive achievements.'   (Ward 1977)

Ward emphasizes here the importance of considering solutions in terms of what they offer the individual client, in order to realize a social work approach to residential care. She suggests that, if this view is taken, then 'institutionalisation' must be seen as 'the blockage crippling residential work' because it is a residential solution which is unconcerned with the individual resident and is therefore at odds with social work values. In contrast, residential intervention is clearly the way in which residential work fits most closely with social work because it is a goal-directed strategy concerned with individual change. Residential care, too, with its emphasis on individual fulfilment, is in harmony with social work values, even if its operation may not necessarily require the skills of trained social workers.

If this, or a similar framework, is used to marry residential work and outcomes with social work values and methods, then the areas of future expansion and contraction become identifiable. Whether units offer family-substitute, family-alternative or family-supplement care, they should aim to pursue practices which maximize individual change and fulfilment. Those units which do not are unacceptable as a part of residential social work.

Let us turn next to a consideration of the financial arguments for contraction. It is apparent that the growing preoccupation in the 1970s with the rising costs of residential care has also promoted the view that a reduction in the scope of residential provision needs to take place.

This is not, by any means, a recent preoccupation. Residential care is the most costly personal social services provision and its history has been peppered at regular intervals by financial considerations. Scull's investigation of the evolution of nineteenth-century asylum care for the mentally disordered in Britain provides an early case study of the way in which financial concerns have influenced the range of British residential solutions. He suggests that an outstanding feature of the original blueprints for asylum care, pioneered by such practitioners as John Connolly, was an emphasis on the importance of developing regimes which were provided in small 'household' size units and concerned with a homely, individualized response to patient need. He goes on to demonstrate how the possibility of realizing these blueprints was rapidly undermined by preoccupations with saving ratepayers' money through realizing economies of scale in large, regimented institutions (Scull 1979 : 117).

A similar pattern can be traced in the post-war development of local authority residential units for elderly people. As Townsend points out, the notion of transforming this area of care from workhouse provision into small homes became increasingly unpopular as the costs involved became apparent (Townsend 1964). The consequence was a slow and uneven transformation in which larger homes were built than had at first been proposed. When the financial implications of continuing to provide this kind of care for an expanding elderly population began to emerge more clearly, questions were raised about the policy as a whole. As Bosanquet puts it: '(While) many doubts have been expressed in the last twenty years about the desirability of these homes . . . it has been the brute force of spending restrictions which has been the most significant brake on the building of these homes' (Bosanquet 1978 : 111).

It is likely that such restrictions will continue to be an important feature of the welfare services in Britain in the immediate future. Currently it is estimated that half of a local authority social services department's budget is spent on the provision of residential care (DHSS 1975). This being so, it is easy to see how the anti-institutional arguments of the professionals will feed into the attempts of central and local government representatives and managers to justify reductions in expenditure in this area. The costs of residential care are known and rising, the costs of its alternatives – vaguely defined as 'community care' – are often hidden and negotiable. There is, therefore, apparent complementarity between the economic considerations which will underlie any future contraction of residential care and the professional ones which are reflected in the argument for a limited use of residential solutions.

It is also likely that answers in the future to the question of how much residential care is needed and for whom, will be heavily influenced by this fusion of anti-institutional and financial considerations. If this proves to be the case, it is important to attempt to assess the likely outcomes of contraction for residential workers, potential residents, and their families.

Possible outcomes

Let us consider overall contraction first. The pattern outlined by Righton and others is one in which the needs of thousands of individuals currently being met by the use of residential care are reassessed and met by the co-ordinated use of alternative resources in the community.

How likely is this change to take place? Co-ordination and availability of these resources is an essential element in this strategy yet present trends do not suggest that there are grounds to be optimistic about either of them in the near future. There are currently considerable problems in co-ordinating services within, as well as between, the large bureaucratic organizations responsible for providing public welfare in Britain. Recent changes in both the organization and legislative framework of the health service, local authority housing, and the income maintenance services, probably mean that contraction of residential provision which dovetails with the provision of alternative community-based resources is unlikely.

As for the availability (co-ordinated or otherwise) of alternative community-based resources, these are already subject to the same kind of financial restraints which face the residential services and, in such circumstances, it may be impossible for them to respond adequately to a contraction in residential provision.

If these difficulties in responding to any contraction of residential services do occur, then it is likely that it will be the 'natural' networks of family and community which will be left to care for those for whom residential provision is no longer available. If increased demands are made on family and community care a number of issues are likely to emerge.

The research to date, which has tried to identify what is meant by community care, suggests that 'in practice community care equals care by the family, and in practice care by the family equals care by women' (Finch and Groves 1980 : 494). Community and family care is care, in other words, provided in the main by adult women as part of their domestic responsibilities. Wilkins's study of mentally handicapped children at home (Wilkins 1979), Bayley's study of the community care of mentally handicapped adults (Bayley 1973), and Hunt's study of handicapped elderly people (Hunt 1978), all demonstrate how it is women as relatives, friends, and neighbours, who provide the bulk of care for these groups living in the community.

This being so, any contraction of residential care linked to an increased reliance on family and community care will add to the pressures made on women to spend their time at home in unpaid domestic labour. At a period when an increasing number of women, particularly married women, are choosing to leave their homes in order to take paid work, these demands are likely to raise conflicts. Unless the women concerned are able to shift the patterns of work-sharing within their own households, they are likely to be left spending longer periods housebound, engaged in caring for dependants, than they might otherwise have chosen. How acceptable this will be to them will depend on the social and economic conditions they and their families find themselves in. It will also depend on the individual expectations they have of their adult lives. Their responses to their predicament will have considerable implications for the way in which any contraction of state residential care is experienced by thousands of individuals. As Finch and Groves argue, these responses are likely to be of interest to policy makers; for with current levels of unemployment, women who have dependent relatives may find that they are subjected to increased social and cultural pressures to give up paid employment and stay at home as carers. Such action would be seen as freeing jobs for others and providing what is considered by government to be a 'low cost' solution to the need for care (Finch and Groves 1980).

For groups of potential residents who do not have family and friends to fall back on, a contraction of residential care without an adequate expansion of alternative welfare resources is likely to have equally important implications. We are already witnessing what some of these might be. The reduction of long-stay psychiatric hospital provision which has taken place in Britain over the last fifteen years or so has resulted in thousands of individuals with very limited resources competing in the private market for housing and board and lodging accommodation. The poverty of their lives, both materially and socially, raises fundamental questions about some of the consequences of contracting residential care without ensuring the availability of adequate alternatives. Perhaps there is something to be learned here from the more extended American experience of the same phenomena; experiences which have currently resulted in attempts to begin to re-think the policy of 'de-institutionalization' (Scull 1977).

The contraction of our current residential services is an option which, if chosen will also have consequences for those who use the new services. The idea of limiting residential care to a smaller number of residents is likely to change the nature of the residential task itself. Several commentators, for example, Hoghughi, suggest that such a shift will inevitably leave staff caring for groups of highly disturbed or dependent residents who are regarded as risks to themselves and others in the community. The demands made on residential workers by these groups will differ from the demands currently made in most residential units, and therefore the focus of residential work and the skills and techniques required are bound to change (Hoghughi 1978).

The other aspect of contraction which needs to be taken into account is the selection process which will be used to identify those suitable for this limited, intensive care. The problems of classification and selection have dogged residential care since its inception. It appears to be virtually impossible for most units to reach a point where staff feel satisfied that they are working with the 'right kind' of resident. It is as if staff dissatisfaction with the characteristics displayed by residents is an almost inevitable feature of residential work. Some staff invoke the memory of a 'golden age' in their working lives, when the children they cared for were not so disturbed, or their elderly residents were not so frail, or their handicapped residents were not so deteriorated. Others feel that they have never been able to use their skills as they would like to and suggest that this is because the kind of residents who need those skills are never 'sent their way'. However it is expressed, this apparent failure to select satisfactorily continues to be viewed as a key problem by residential staff.

In a situation where there is an attempt to restrict the use of residential care to a small minority, who cannot be settled in the community, this problem is likely to become even more considerable. How and when in the case of any individual is it possible to establish that failure to settle in the community reflects a need for intensive residential care? How do such circumstances differ from those in which it is clear that there is a need for more adequate and effective community welfare resources? Here we come back to the difficulty raised in chapter six, of separating individual need for residential care from a failure of alternative social situations to offer adequate care to the individual concerned. What may make this problem particularly significant is that a residential care system which is known to be limited to a 'hard core' of 'difficult' individuals, is bound to be highly stigmatizing. The consequences of having a history as a resident in such a system are likely to be keenly felt in any individual's subsequent life. Because of this, justifying the choice of such an experience for anyone would be critical for those social workers who become involved in making that choice.

The suggestion is, then, that if the option of limiting the scope of state residential care is pursued without a compensatory increase in the co-ordinated use of community-based welfare services, then families, clients, and residential workers, will be faced with at least three major changes to respond to. First, families (or more probably adult women in families) are likely to meet an increase in the expectation that they will provide care for dependent relatives for prolonged periods of their lives. Second, clients without the option of family care, may find that the major available alternative to a highly stigmatized state care system, is very materially and socially deprived community living. Third, residential workers are likely to find themselves working in units which, in catering for 'disturbed' and 'highly dependent' resident groups, begin to pursue residential tasks making very different demands on staff.

Let us turn now to the second outcome which is currently being canvassed in the professional literature. What is the likelihood that in the near future the residential task will, in practice, move closer to social work? The answers being given to this question reflect the division between optimists, pessimists, and radicals, discussed in chapter one.

From the optimists' viewpoint, Elliott, in a recent overview of some of the factors likely to change the nature of the residential task, concludes: 'the mirage of an increasingly skilled and specialized task, which is fully integrated into the continuum of services and glimpsed by residential workers for many years, is becoming more of a reality' (Walton and Elliott 1980 : 22). The reasons that she gives for her optimism are the spread of new ideas in residential practice and theory; the effects of changes in residential populations; the improvement in conditions of service; and the availability of training for residential workers. In her view, the key worker concept which extends the boundaries of the task, the increasing focus in social work theory on social as well as individual explanation, and the increasing acceptance in practice of resident participation, are all likely to be significant in changing the nature of residential social work. Alongside this, effects of changes in the population structure, the emphasis on fostering and other community alternatives for potential residents, and an increased awareness of the needs of the disabled, are likely, in her view, to result in more 'difficult' and 'frail' residents entering care who will demand a more skilled and specialist response from workers.

As for conditions of work and training, Elliott argues that the recent limit on the length of the working week and improvement in salaries has moved residential workers closer to their field work colleagues. The result is an increased professional standing for the work, as well as an increase in the numbers of staff working in each establishment. Changes in the structure of training now offers the possibility that inroads can be made on the 96 per cent of residential staff who currently hold no relevant qualification.

Elliott acknowledges that there are problems in moving forward in all these areas. The key worker concept, for example, has received little public attention, whilst the two-tier pattern of training on its present scale is likely to have only a marginal impact on training needs. But, on balance, she sees such changes as influencing the future of the service in a positive direction.

For the optimists, generally, the training of residential workers is the key to realizing the kind of residential care and residential intervention that Ward describes. Jones (1979), Righton (1977), Ward (Walton and Elliott 1980 : 25), and others, all emphasize that it is the attitudes and practices of residential staff which determine the quality of the residential solutions offered; it has been this contribution to residential provision which has traditionally been neglected. It is Righton's view that while the vast majority of those working in residential care remain untrained, 'what should be one of the greatest positives will remain an obstructive and obstinate negative'.

At current rates (and there seems little likelihood of expansion of training in the near future) it seems unlikely that the percentage of qualified workers in the service will rise very rapidly. The two-tier nature of training raises further uncertainties about the spread of qualifications, as there is already some evidence that relatively few residential workers are being seconded for CQSW training (Walton and Elliott 1980).

If training continues to have such a limited impact, then realizing a transformation, at least in principle, in the nature of residential care is dependent on the effectiveness of the social work profession as a pressure group on central and local government policy and financial decisions. The current ambivalence demonstrated towards residential care by the profession does not suggest that this will be easy to achieve.

For the pessimists, there appears to be little in the current or future situation to suggest that any positive changes in this area are likely. Indeed, there are a number of negative indicators. In their view, a Britain faced with a continuing economic crisis is likely to generate an increasing number of the kind of social, economic, and psychological difficulties which result in the breakdown of individuals and families and an increased demand for state residential solutions. In this situation they consider that it is more, rather than less, likely that the pressures to use residential units as 'containers' for those posing problems for society will increase.

If this proves to be the case, then there is only a marginal chance that a profession, likely to find itself under criticism for failing to cope with an increasing number of social problems, will be able to begin to swing the residential services away from institutionalization and towards residential care and intervention. It is also unlikely that these circumstances will shift the dominant assumptions about the relationship between residential care and the family, which pessimists identify as the source of the current stigma and low status associated with residential solutions. The conclusions being reached here are that the residential services, whether they are reduced in size or not, will find themselves under increased pressure to contain problems. In responding to this pressure they will retain their predominantly 'institutionalizing' tendencies.

In contrast with this vision of workers and residents continuing to be trapped in a stigmatizing, poor quality service, the radicals stress workers' and residents' own potential for fashioning alternative forms of residential experience and fighting for changes in their working and living conditions. This potential is not seen as the product of increased professional training, rather it is seen as the practical outcome of an understanding of the class nature of British society and the function of the family in that society. How workers and residents create the space to explore such alternatives may owe as much to disillusionment and despair with current residential solutions as it does to developing elements already visible in existing practice.

Whatever stance one takes in trying to understand the nature of residential care and predicting its future, one thing is clear. Change has been slow in this area of welfare provision. Where it has taken place it has reflected not only the work of residents and staff but also the contribution of supportive management. In care situations which are publicly accountable new ideas do not develop into new practices if staff feel they will be left to carry the risks involved. For too long residential workers have been expected to cope with situations of intolerable stress and still provide reasonable care. These situations do not just reflect the stresses and strains of daily living, they also reflect a fundamental ambivalence about what state residential solutions should provide for those living and working in them.

Summary

This final chapter has focused on the debate which surrounds the future direction of residential care.

In doing so it has been suggested that there is a degree of complimentarity between professional arguments for a limited residential service and financial concerns about the high costs of residential care.

In considering some of the likely consequences of a contraction of residential care, without a co-ordinated and compensatory use of alternative welfare resources, attention was drawn to the kind of demands which might be made on women relatives, the private housing markets, and residential workers.

The likelihood of moving towards a residential service characterized by a social work approach was considered in terms of the analysis offered in the literature by the optimists, the pessimists, and the radicals. The optimists' emphasis on the importance of professional influence exercised through expanded training programmes and pressure-group activity, was contrasted with the pessimists' emphasis on persistent and overriding structural and ideological influences, and the radicals' stress on the potential of workers and residents to change their own situations.

References

Advisory Council on Child Care (1970) *Care and treatment in a planned environment*. London: ACCC.

Allen, D. (1977) The residential task. Is there one? *Social Work Today* **9** (7).

Apte, R. Z. (1968) *Halfway Houses – a new dilemma in institutional care*. Occasional Papers in Social Administration No. 27. London: Bell.

Arden, N. (1977) *A child of the system*. London: Quartet.

Balberni, R. (1966) *Residential work with children*. Oxford: Pergamon.

Barton, R. (1976) *Institutional neurosis* (3rd edition). Bristol: John Wright.

Bayley, M. (1973) *Mental handicap and community care*. London: Routledge & Kegan Paul.

Bean, P. (1976) *Rehabilitation and deviance*. London: Routledge & Kegan Paul.

Beedell, C. (1970) *Residential life with children*. London: Routledge & Kegan Paul.

Berke, J. H. (1979) *I haven't had to go mad here*. Harmondsworth: Penguin.

Berry, J. (1975) *Daily experience in residential life*. London: Routledge & Kegan Paul.

Bettelheim, B. (1950) *Love is not enough*. New York: The Free Press.

—— (1974) *A home for the heart*. London: Thames & Hudson.

Bosanquet, N. (1978) *A future for old age*. London: Maurice Temple Smith.

Brake, M. and Bailey, R. (eds) (1980) *Radical social work and practice*. London: Edward Arnold.

Brearley, C. P. (1977) *Residential work with the elderly*. London: Routledge & Kegan Paul.

British Association of Social Work (1977) *The social work task*. (Working Party Report). Birmingham: BASW.

Bromley, G. (1977) Interaction between field and residential social workers. *British Journal of Social Work* **7** (3): 346–48.

Brown, M. (ed.) (1974) *Social issues and the social services*. London: Charles Knight.

Bruce, M. (1961) *The coming of the welfare state*. London: Batsford

Carlebach, J. (1970) *Caring for children in trouble*. London: Routledge & Kegan Paul.

Cawson, P. (1978) *Community homes: a study of residential staff*. London: HMSO.

Cawson, P. and Martell, J. (1979) *Children referred to closed units*. London: DHSS.

Central Council for Education and Training in Social Work (CCETSW) Discussion Document (1973a) *Training for residential work*. London: CCETSW.

—— Paper 3 (1973b) Report of working party on education for residential social work. 'Residential work is part of social work.' London: CCETSW.

Central Statistical Office (1978) *Social Trends no. 9*. London: HMSO.

Checkland, S. G. and E. O. A. (eds) (1974) *The Poor Law Report of 1834*. Harmondsworth: Penguin.

Cooper, D. (1970) *Psychiatry and anti-psychiatry*. London: Granada.

Deacon, J. (1974) *Tongue tied*. London: National Society for Mentally Handicapped Children.

DHSS (1971) *Better services for the mentally handicapped*. London: HMSO.

—— (1975) *Health and personal social services statistics for England*. London: HMSO.

—— (1979) *Residential care for the elderly in London*. DHSS Social Work Service, London Region.

Dharamsi, F. *et al.* (1979) *Caring for children and community work. A diary of a local authority children's home*. Ilkley: Owen Wells.

Docker-Drysdale, B. (1973) *Consultation in child care*. Harlow: Longman.

Finch, J. and Groves, D. (1980) Community care and the family: a case for equal opportunities? *Journal of Social Policy* **9** (4): 487–511.

Gill, O. (1974) *Whitegate, an approved school in transition.* Liverpool: Liverpool University Press.

Goffman, E. (1961) *Asylums. Essays on the social situation of mental patients and other inmates.* Harmondsworth: Penguin.

Hansard (1970) *Volume 1407.*

Hinshelwood, R. and Manning, N. (eds) (1979) *Therapeutic communities.* London: Routledge & Kegan Paul.

Hoghughi, M. (1978) *Troubled and troublesome.* London: André Deutsch (Burnett Books).

Holman, R. (1980) *Inequality in child care.* London: Child Poverty Action Group/Family Rights Group.

Hunt, A. (1978) *The elderly at home: a study of people aged 65 and over living in the community in England in 1976.* Social Survey Division, ODCS. London: HMSO.

Jansen, E. (ed.) (1980) *The therapeutic community.* London: Croom Helm.

Jones, H. (1979) *The residential community: a setting for social work.* London: Routledge & Kegan Paul.

Jordan, B. (1974) *Poor parents.* London: Routledge & Kegan Paul.

—— (1976) *Freedom and the welfare state.* London: Routledge & Kegan Paul.

Kahan, B. (1979) *Growing up in care.* Oxford: Blackwell.

Kahan, B. and Banner, G. (1972) *The residential task in child care* (Castle Priory Report). Birmingham: Residential Care Association.

Kammerman, S. B. and Kahan, A. (eds) (1978) *Family policy: Government and families in fourteen countries.* New York: Columbia University Press.

Kew, S. (1975) *Handicap and family crisis.* London: Pitman.

King, R. D., Raynes, N. V., and Tizard, J. (1971) *Patterns of residential care. Sociological studies in institutions for handicapped children.* London: Routledge & Kegan Paul.

Kings Fund Centre (1980) *An ordinary life.* London: KFC.

Lambert, R. and Millham, S. (1968) *The hothouse society.* London: Weidenfeld & Nicolson.

Land, H. and Parker, R. (1978) United Kingdom. In S. B. Kammerman and A. Kahan (eds) *Family policy: Government and families in fourteen countries.* New York: Columbia University Press.

Longmate, N. (1974) *The Workhouse*. London: Maurice Temple Smith.

McCormack, M. (1979) *Away from home. The mentally handicapped in residential care*. London: Constable.

Meacher, M. (1972) *Taken for a ride*. Harlow: Longman.

Menzies, I. E. P. (1960) A case study in the functioning of social systems as a defence against anxiety. *Human Relations* **13**. Reprinted pamphlet 1970. London: Tavistock Institute of Human Relations.

Middleton, N. (1971) *When family failed*. London: Victor Galloway.

Miller, E. J. and Gwynne, G. V. (1972) *A life apart*. London: Tavistock Publications.

Miller, M. (1974) Residential care. *Social Work Today* **5** (9).

Millham, S., Bullock, R., and Cherrett, P. (1975) *After teeth grace: comparative study of the experience of boys in approved school*. London: Human Context Books.

Millham, S., Bullock, R., and Hosie, K. (1978) Another try. In N. Tutt (ed.) *Alternative strategies for coping with crime*. Oxford: Blackwell and Martin Robertson.

Moroney, R. M. (1976) *The family and the state. Considerations for social policy*. Harlow: Longman.

Morris, P. (1969) *Put away*. London: Routledge & Kegan Paul.

Newson, J. and E. (1968) *Four years old in an urban community*. London: Allen & Unwin.

—— (1976) *Seven years old in the home environment*. London: Allen & Unwin.

Newton, E. (1980) *This bed my centre*. London: Virago.

Oswin, M. (1973) *The empty hours*. Harmondsworth: Penguin.

Packman, J. (1975) *The child's generation*. Oxford: Blackwell and Martin Robertson.

Paige, R. and Clarke, G. (eds) (1977) *Who cares?* London: National Children's Bureau.

Parsloe, P. and Stevenson, O. (1979) *Social service teams*. London: HMSO.

Payne, C. (1977) Residential social work. In H. Specht and A. Vickery (eds) *Integrated social work methods*. London: Allen & Unwin.

Payne, C. and White, K. (1979) *Caring for deprived children*. London: RCA/Croom Helm.

Personal Social Services Council (1975) *Living and working in residential homes*. London: PSSC.

—— (1977) *Residential care reviewed*. London: PSSC.

Race, D. G. and Race, D. M. (1979) *The Cherries Group home: a beginning*. London: HMSO.

Raynes, N., Pratt, M., and Roses, S. (1979) *Organisational structure and the care of the mentally retarded*. London: Croom Helm.

Report of care and children committee (The Curtis Report) (1946) Cmnd. 6922. London: HMSO.

Report of the committee on children and young persons (1960) Cmnd. 1191. London: HMSO.

Report of the committee on local authority and allied personal social services (The Seebohm Report) (1968) Cmnd. 3703. London: HMSO.

Report of the committee of enquiry into mental handicap, nursing and care (The Jay Report) (1979) Cmnd. 7468. London: HMSO.

Residential Care Association and the British Association of Social Workers (1976) The relationship between field and residential work. *Social Work Today* **7** (12).

Residential Care Association (1977) The residential task. *Social Work Today* **9** (1).

Righton, P. (1976) It's a battleground. *Social Work Today* **8** (3).

—— (1977) Positive and negative aspects of residential care. *Social Work Today* **8** (37).

Rowe, J. and Lambert, L. (1973) *Children who wait*. London: Association of British Adoption Agencies.

Schorr, A. L. (ed.) (1975) *Children and decent people*. London: Allen & Unwin.

Scull, A. T. (1977) *Decarceration: community treatment and the deviant a radical view*. Englewood Cliffs: Prentice Hall.

—— (1979) *Museums of madness*. London: Allen & Unwin.

Shenfield, B. (1957) *Social policies for old age*. London: Routledge & Kegan Paul.

Sinclair, I. (1971) *Hostels for probationers*. Home Office Research Study No. 6. London: HMSO.

Taylor, L., Lacey, R., and Bracken, D. (1980) *In whose best interests?* London: The Cobden Trust/MIND.

Tizard, J., Sinclair, I., and Clarke, R. V. G. (eds) (1975) *Varieties of residential experience*. London: Routledge & Kegan Paul.

Towell, D. and Harries, C. (1979) *Innovations in patient care*. London: Croom Helm.

Townsend, M. (1977) *The need for care: A census of residents in homes for the elderly*. London: Social Work Advisory Group, DHSS.

Townsend, P. (1964) *The last refuge*. London: Routledge & Kegan Paul.

—— (1973) *The social minority*. Harmondsworth: Penguin.

Tutt, N. (ed.) (1978) *Alternative strategies for coping with crime*. Oxford: Blackwell and Martin Robertson.

Twining, L. (1898) *Work houses and pauperism*. Harlow: Longman.

Wagner, G. (1979) *Barnardo*. London: Weidenfeld & Nicolson.

Walton, R. G. and Elliott, D. (eds) (1980) *Residential care. A reader in current theory and practice*. Oxford: Pergamon.

Ward, L. (1977) Clarifying the residential social work task. *Social Work Today* **9** (2).

Wilkins, D. (1979) *Caring for the mentally handicapped child*. London: Croom Helm.

The Williams Report (1967) *Caring for people: staffing residential homes*. London: Allen & Unwin.

Wills, D. (1971) *Spare the child*. Harmondsworth: Penguin.

Wilson, E. (1977) *Women and the welfare state*. London: Tavistock Publications.

Wing, J. K. and Brown, G. W. (1970) *Institutionalism and schizophrenia. A comparative study of three mental hospitals*. Cambridge: Cambridge University Press.

Women's Group on Public Welfare (1948) *The neglected child and his family*. Oxford: Oxford University Press.

Younghusband, E. (1978) *Social work in Britain 1950–1975*. Vols 1 and 2. London: Allen & Unwin.

Index

Name index

Subject index

148   The Residential Solution